Introduction

When we look at a famous painting, we inevitably concentrate on the central figure, event or theme of the picture. This, after all, is what the artist intended us to focus on.

But in traditional realist painting, the subject is presented in a specific context - which may vary from a simple coloured surface or deep shadow to an involved and detailed space. Of course, this space has been chosen to support and explain further the meaning of the picture. So at the end of the day, a background is just that - a background. Yet in many great paintings, that background - when isolated and looked at as an image in itself - can often reveal a further level of thinking on the part of the artist that might easily be overlooked in a casual, or too literal reading of the image.

The basic intention of this book is simply to draw attention to some of the fascinating details that underpin many great and famous images in western art. The illustrations consist of pencil and watercolour sketches by the author from the selected paintings. They are not meant to be accurate copies in any sense - they are simply brief evocations which I enjoyed doing and learned a great deal about the paintings in the process. I hope you enjoy looking at these images as much as I did, and if they stimulate just one person to go and look (or look again) at the works in question, then the exercise will have been worthwhile.

Contents

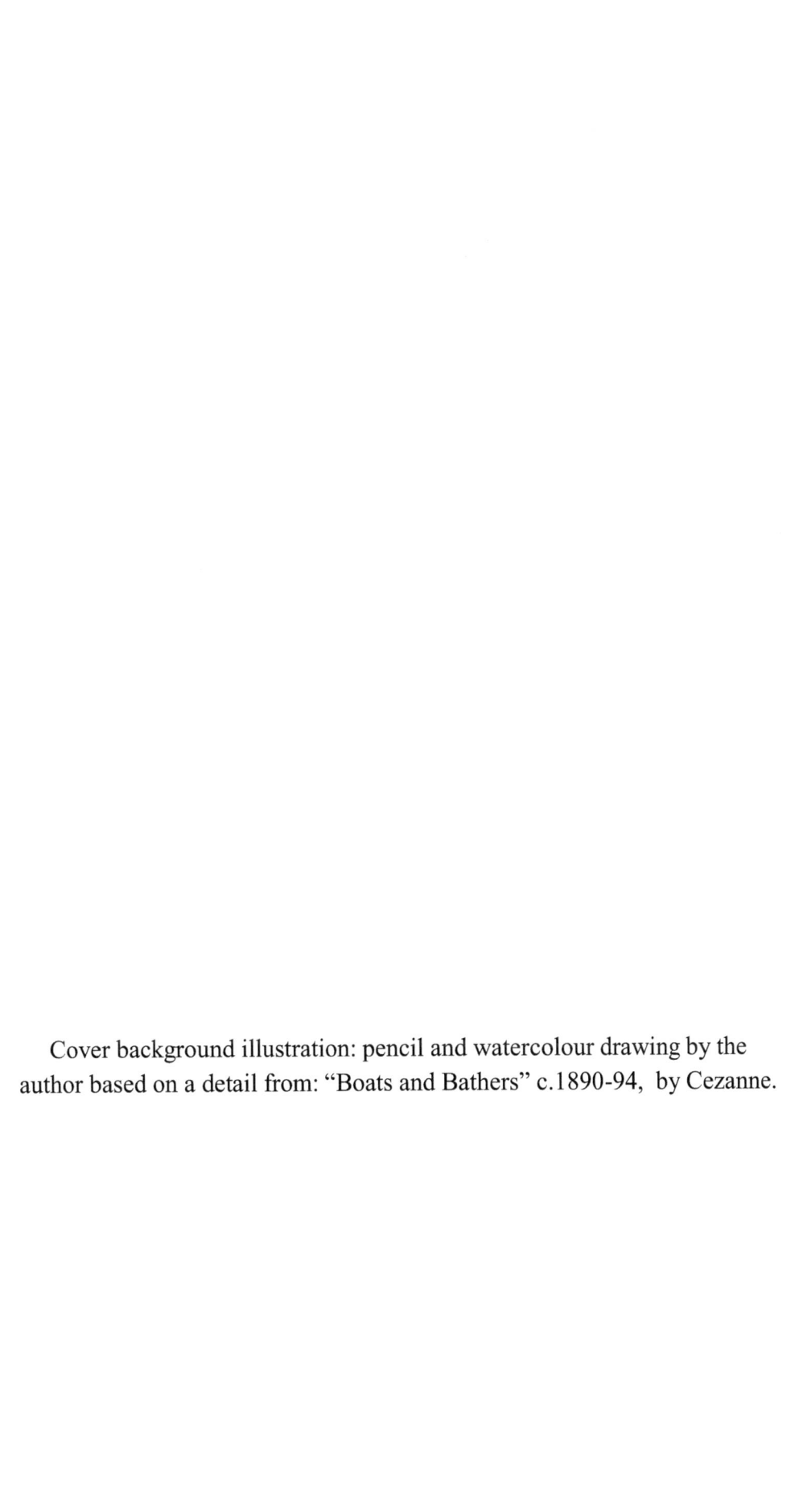

1. Giotto di Bondone (1267?-1337) <u>or:</u>

Master of the Legend of St. Francis (active late 13thc.)

St. Francis giving his coat to a poor man, c. 1300

Basilca of St. Francis, Assisi

Traditionally, it was assumed that Giotto, the most important of the early Florentine masters who is often seen as a precursor of the Italian Renaissance, had painted the cycle of frescoes of the legend of St. Francis in the upper church at Assisi. Nowadays, many scholars disagree, but the fact remains that whoever painted them shared Giotto's ability to break free, at least as far as his figures are concerned, from the flat, cut-out images of the old Byzantine and medieval traditions, and render the human form as rounded and solid. Vasari, in his Lives of the Painters, Sculptors and Architects, is clearly convinced that these frescoes were by Giotto, who he tells us "…..studied Nature diligently, and was always…..borrowing ideas from her". Whether that is true of the landscape background in this picture is debatable. Rather, it remains close to the stereotyped renderings of landscape that were found in late medieval manuscript illumination. The buildings are broadly summarized, the rocky hills are formulaic, and the vegetation is almost childlike in its simplicity. Nevertheless, the artist presents us with a delicately enchanting image of an imaginary Italian hill town.

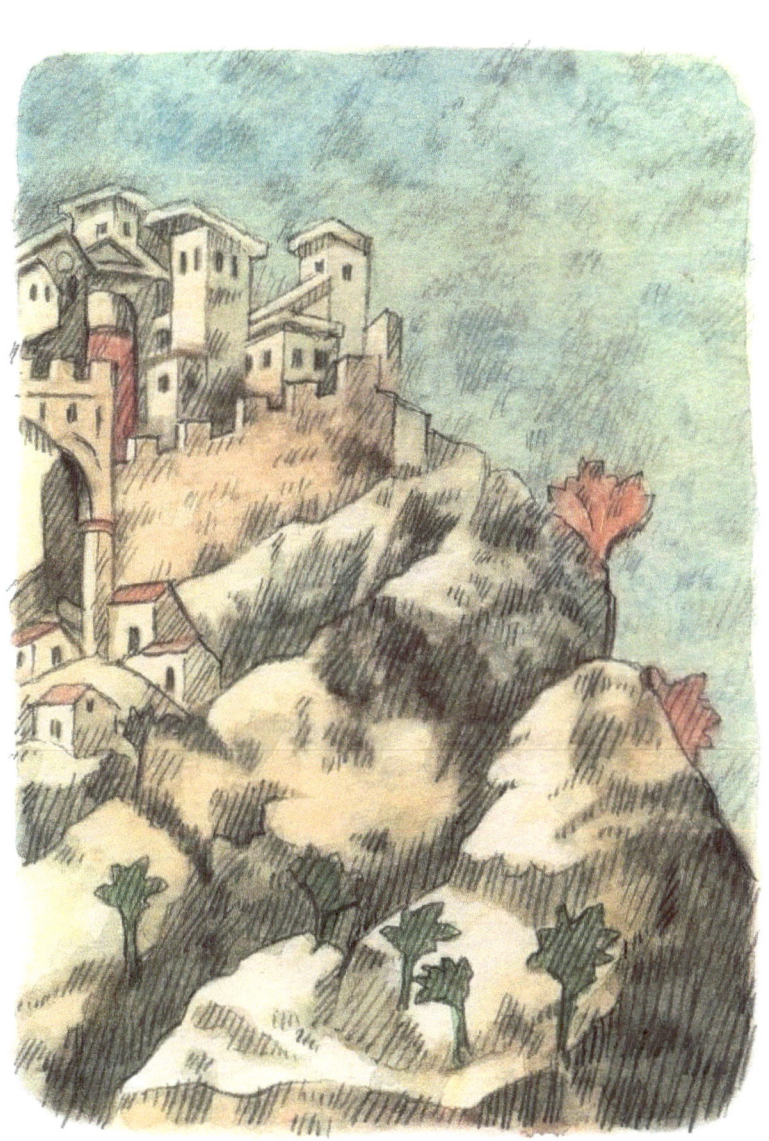

2. Limbourg brothers (died 1416)

Tres Riches Heures du Duc de Berry

"December" c. 1412 – 1416

Musee Conde, Chantilly

The Tres Riches Heures is a Book of Hours, that is a collection of prayers which comprises a series of illustrations of the months, the most remarkable of which were painted by the brothers Limbourg. Although they were born in the Netherlands, they produced this their most famous work at the court of the Duc de Berry in Burgundy. Left unfinished at the death of both brothers (possibly from the plague) in 1416, it was completed later by the French illuminator Jean Colombe and others. It is widely regarded as almost the last, but at the same time one of the most glorious late flowerings of the medieval "International Gothic" style. The colours are glowing, even jewel-like, but what sets it apart from the Gothic tradition is the beautifully rendered space in the illustrations. The calendar images illustrate everyday events of the period - this one, December, features a wild boar hunt. The background presents a frieze of woodland beyond which we see some glimpses of splendid Gothic towers which may be the Duke's lavish Chateau de Vincennes. Though the trees are rather schematic and the image as a whole has the appearance of a theatrical backdrop, nevertheless the overall feeling of actual air and atmosphere is thoroughly convincing.

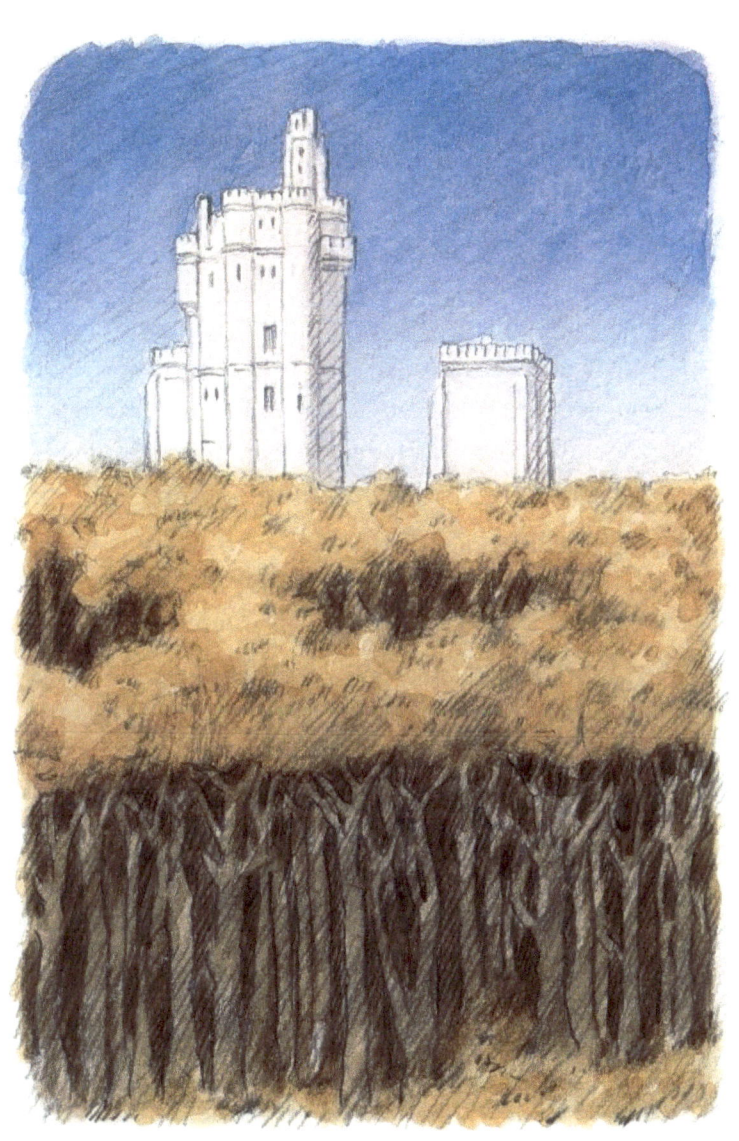

3. Giovanni Bellini (c. 1430-1516)

Woman at her Toilet 1515

Vienna, Kunsthistorisches Museum

Giovanni Bellini is said to have learned the technique of oil painting from his contemporary Antonello da Messina, who was working in Bellini's home city of Venice, but he took it to a level never seen before. This painting, of a woman with a mirror, which may be a portrait but is probably an allegory of female beauty, is characteristically suffused with a gentle golden light, which extends into the landscape glimpsed through the window. This landscape, like the figure herself, is idealized and partly imaginary. But Bellini's use of rich colouring and clear light makes it feel quite credible and convincing. The picture was painted towards the end of his life, but the light and colour are as clear as in his earlier Madonnas, which so strongly influenced the two younger masters of Venetian colour, Giorgione and Titian. The scene out of the window, which by this time was a well-established convention in early Renaissance painting, is of course merely a background. Yet this image, with its soft atmospheric light and subtle colouring, could easily stand as an independent landscape painting evocative of the hill towns and mountains of northern Italy.

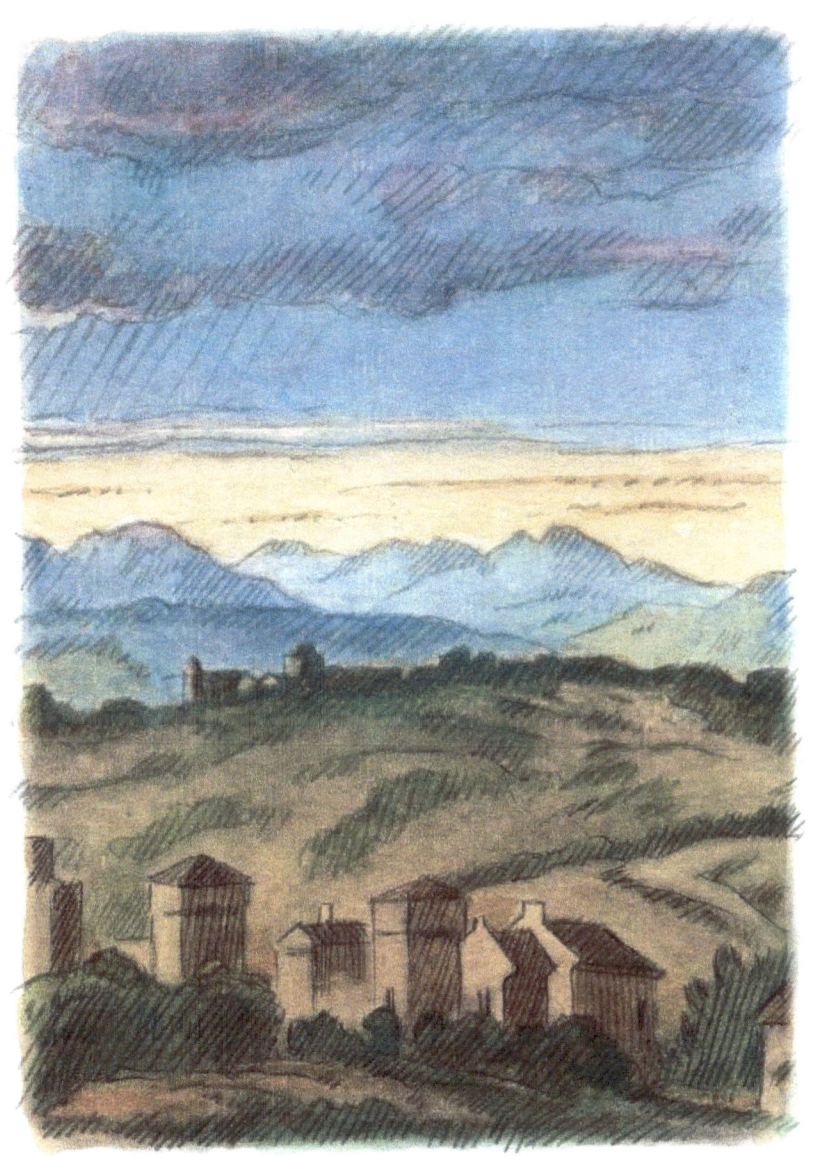

4. Giorgione (c. 1477-1510)

Concert Champetre c. 1508-10

Louvre, Paris

Giorgione's painting of a musical party out in the fields and woods is almost the definition of a painted idyll - a dream or fantasy of life as it might have been in some distant, Arcadian past. The actual meaning of the picture as a whole has never been convincingly explained. Why are the two men, wearing contemporary clothing, accompanied by two nude (or very nearly so) women? Very little is known about Giorgione - only a handful of paintings are accepted as definitely his own work - but one agreed fact seems to be that he loved music. Perhaps, then, the likeliest explanation is that the painting is an allegory of music, with the nudes representing the muses or inspiration to the young men. But certainly it shares the soft, atmospheric character that can be found in all of his paintings. The format of the picture, and the placing of the figures, seem to invite us to look into the central prospect, where we find an almost enchanted evocation of a hilltop farm and a valley stretching far away into the distance. This particular image seems, in fact, to have much more in common with the work of Giorgione's pupil Titian, who is known to have finished the painting after Giorgione' untimely death from the plague.

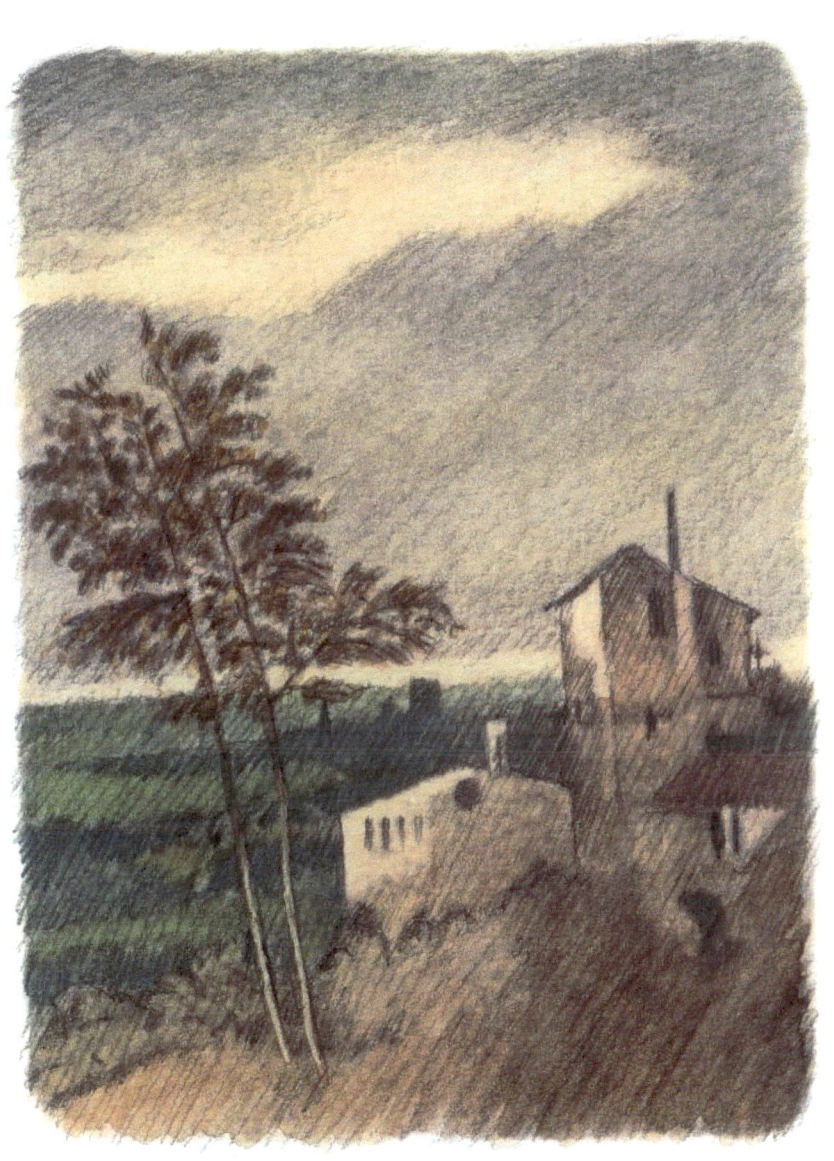

5. Palma Vecchio (c. 1480-1528)

Venus and Cupid c. 1525

Fitzwilliam Museum, Cambridge

Though not born in Venice, Palma Vecchio was very much a Venetian painter, a pupil of Giovanni Bellini, and undoubtedly a great admirer of Giorgione. He excelled at painting voluptuous nudes - especially blondes and fair-haired models painted for private patrons. This picture is no exception, where Venus seems to be more interested in languidly showing off her sensuous charms than paying attention to Cupid and his arrow. She is reclining in a rocky grotto, but if we look beyond the figures we find that almost a third of the picture is devoted to an extensive view of an impressive hill town, with another smaller settlement glimpsed down in the valley, dominated in the distance by a range of craggy mountains. Although earth colours proliferate on the ground, the pale yellows and deep blues of the sky are still vibrant, despite the inevitable deterioration over the centuries.

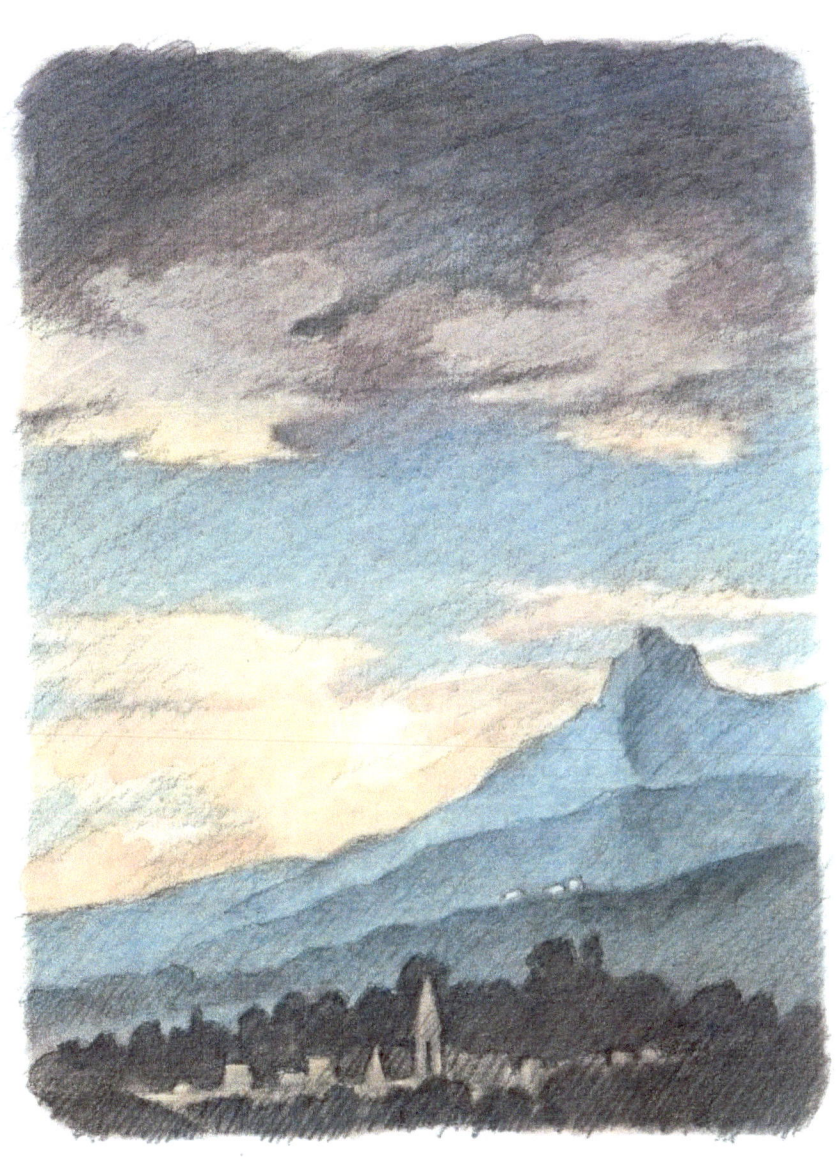

6. Leonardo da Vinci (1452-1519)

The Virgin of the Rocks c. 1491-1508

National Gallery, London

Even in his own day, Leonardo was regarded as a unique genius unlike any other. His achievements in science, anatomy, military hardware etc. are legendary, but it is his legacy as a painter that has impressed so many subsequent generations. Yet this painting raises a number of baffling questions. Principally: why would an artist who was a famously slow worker and who frequently failed to complete paintings have produced two finished versions of the same subject, separated by up to two decades? This one in London appears to be the second version, the first is in the Louvre, Paris, and they are very similar, though not identical. In both, the Virgin and Child with the infant John the Baptist and an angel are in a strange rocky grotto leading through to a distant valley with further fantastic rocky hills and crags. No less intriguing is why Leonardo chose to set the sacred group in this almost surreal landscape. There have been several theories, but we know from his notebooks that he was fascinated by dramatic geological phenomena, so he may have simply seized upon the subject as an excuse to use his knowledge of rock formations. That apart, the painting, particularly its background, perfectly illustrates his two greatest technical innovations, i.e. "sfumato", or the softening of edges, and aerial perspective, particularly colour changes over distance.

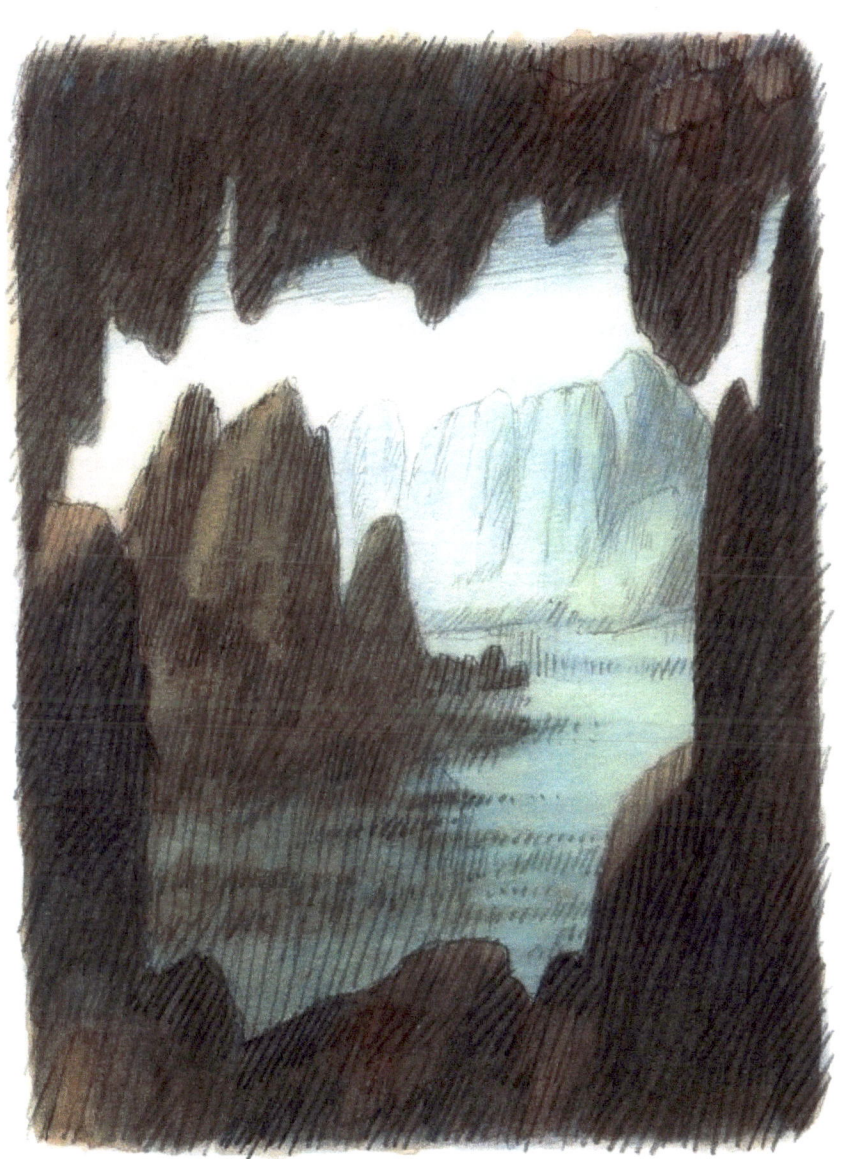

7. Albrecht Durer (1471-1528)

The Adoration of the Magi 1504

Uffizi, Florence

Durer was fascinated by old crumbling classical ruins. He returned to them many times in the backgrounds of some of his paintings and prints. It is unlikely that Durer actually saw anything remotely similar to this during his youth in Northern Europe - although he is generally regarded as German, and considered Nuremberg to be his home town, he was in fact born in Hungary. But by 1505 he had travelled across the Alps to Italy twice, and been impressed by the great Venetian painters such as Giovanni Bellini, as well as impressing many of his Italian contemporaries himself. The Italian artists were particularly impressed by Durer's sure rendering of fine detail, which may have owed much to his early mastery of engraving. In fact, however, there is not much specific detail in this background, apart from a few round-headed arches (which could in fact be north European Romanesque rather than Roman). But it is not really about archaeological accuracy - it is a setting, a dream of somewhere warm and mellow and far away, where a very special baby just might have been born in a sunny, imaginary landscape.

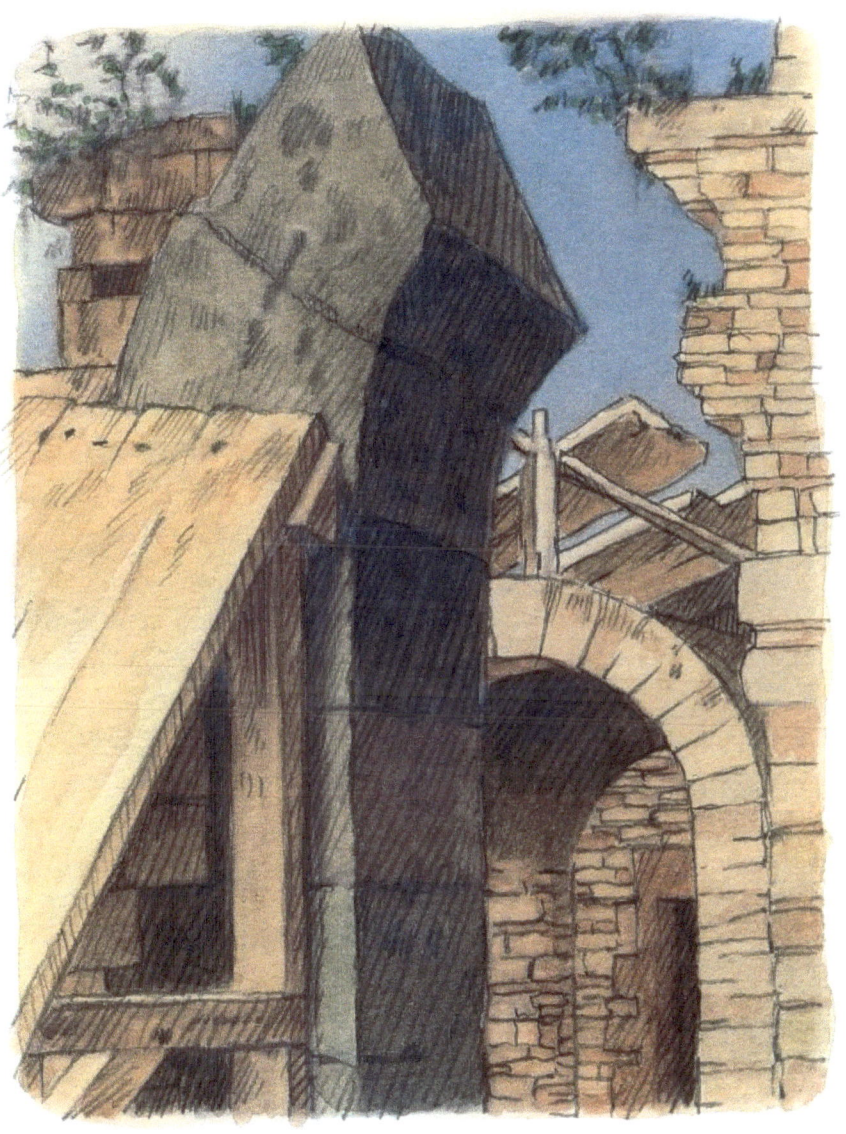

8. Primaticcio (1504-70)

Ulysses and Penelope c. 1545

Toledo, Museum of Arts

This painting is related to one of the many decorative panels produced by Primaticcio and other Italian artists, including Rosso Fiorentino, for the French King Francis I at Fontainebleau. Primaticcio was an exact contemporary of Parmigianino and, though one was born in Bologna and the other in Parma, together they came to typify the style of painting referred to as early Mannerism - a loose movement that set out to overturn the "rules" of the art of High Renaissance masters such as Raphael. One of the ways they did this was to distort the proportions of the human body, frequently making their figures strangely slender and elongated. This is seen in the background here, where two odd and sinister-looking silhouettes are framed against a soft evening sky seen through a tall archway. Whether they are in any way related to the main figures in the composition is ambiguous - they simply appear to be enacting a strange and inexplicable drama of their own in a dim distance.

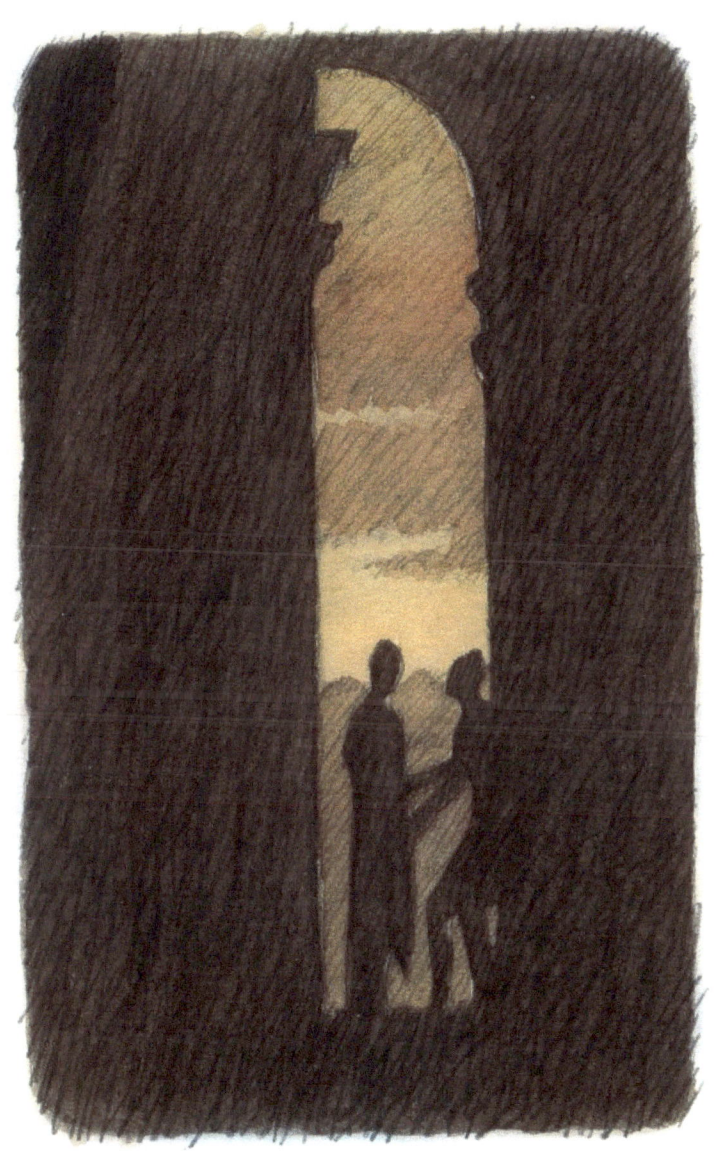

9. Pieter Bruegel (c. 1525-69)

Hunters in the Snow 1565

Kunsthistorisches Museum, Vienna

Bruegel is probably most famous for his amusing paintings of peasant life in the Netherlands of the sixteenth century. But for many, his finest work is landscape, especially his great series "The Seasons", from which this is his evocation of winter. The picture as a whole presents us with an entire series of everyday episodes that we see played out across an extensive landscape of valley and hills. But the bare trees, the humble snow-covered cottages, the distant woods and mountains, and the heavy, threatening sky are almost unique within their era for their stark realism. Yet, atmospheric as it is, the painting as a whole is not pure naturalism - there is incident and anecdote, as always with Bruegel. While his peasant subjects are very much of his time, his landscapes are more timeless; they look both forward and back - back to the exquisite landscapes in some late medieval manuscript illuminations such as the "Tres Riches Heures" of the Limbourg brothers, and forward to the heroic landscape vision of the Romantics.

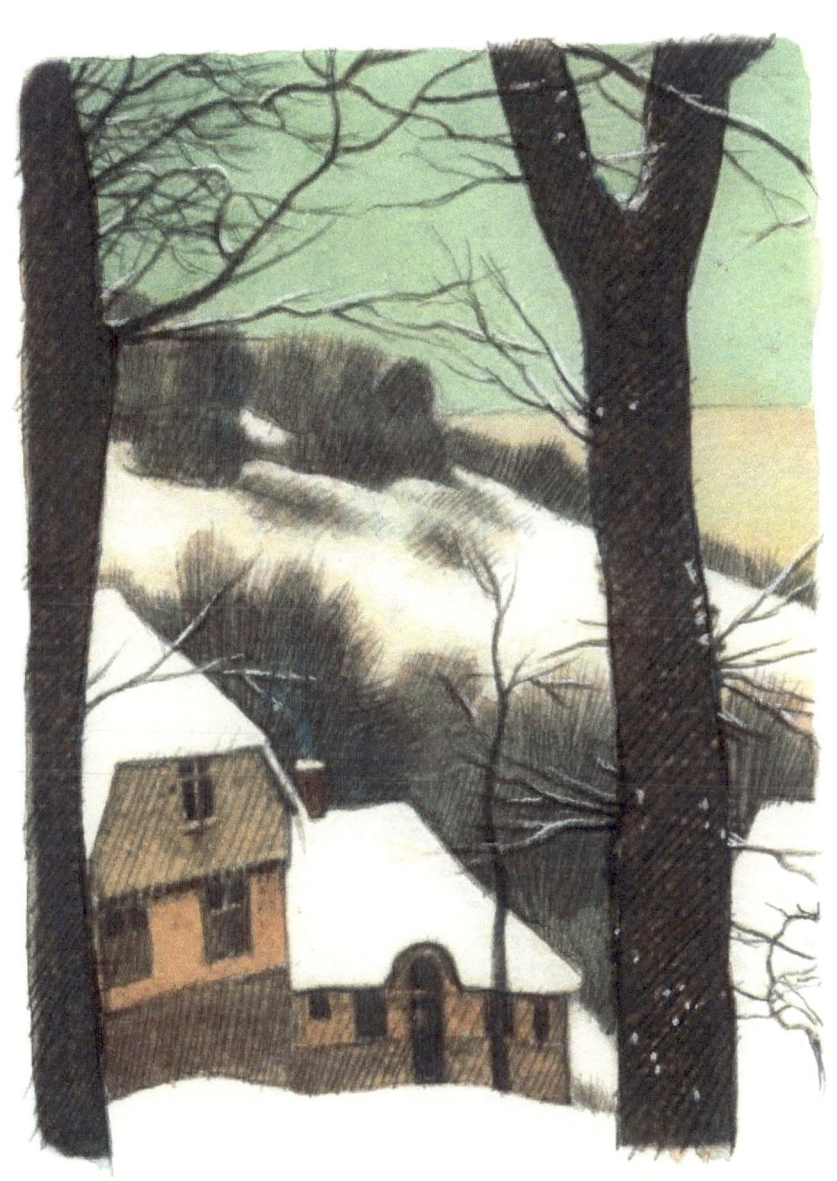

10. Nicolas Poussin (1594-1665)

Christ and the woman taken in adultery 1653

Louvre, Paris

Although he was born in France, Poussin spent most of his adult life in Rome. He was fascinated by classical architecture, therefore he was drawn to Greek and Roman history and poetry throughout his life. Even in a Biblical subject like this, he can not resist depicting it in a grand, monumental architectural setting. Poussin's approach to painting was very methodical and was dominated by theories based on his study of Antiquity. Even his landscapes, which were revered by Cezanne more than two hundred years later, were meticulously planned, often based on table-top models that he constructed beforehand. As a result of all this, his figures often seem stiff and unlife-like to modern eyes. On the other hand, many of the details in his pictures, as in this illustration, have a clarity and precision that could almost be compared with some aspects of twentieth century abstraction.

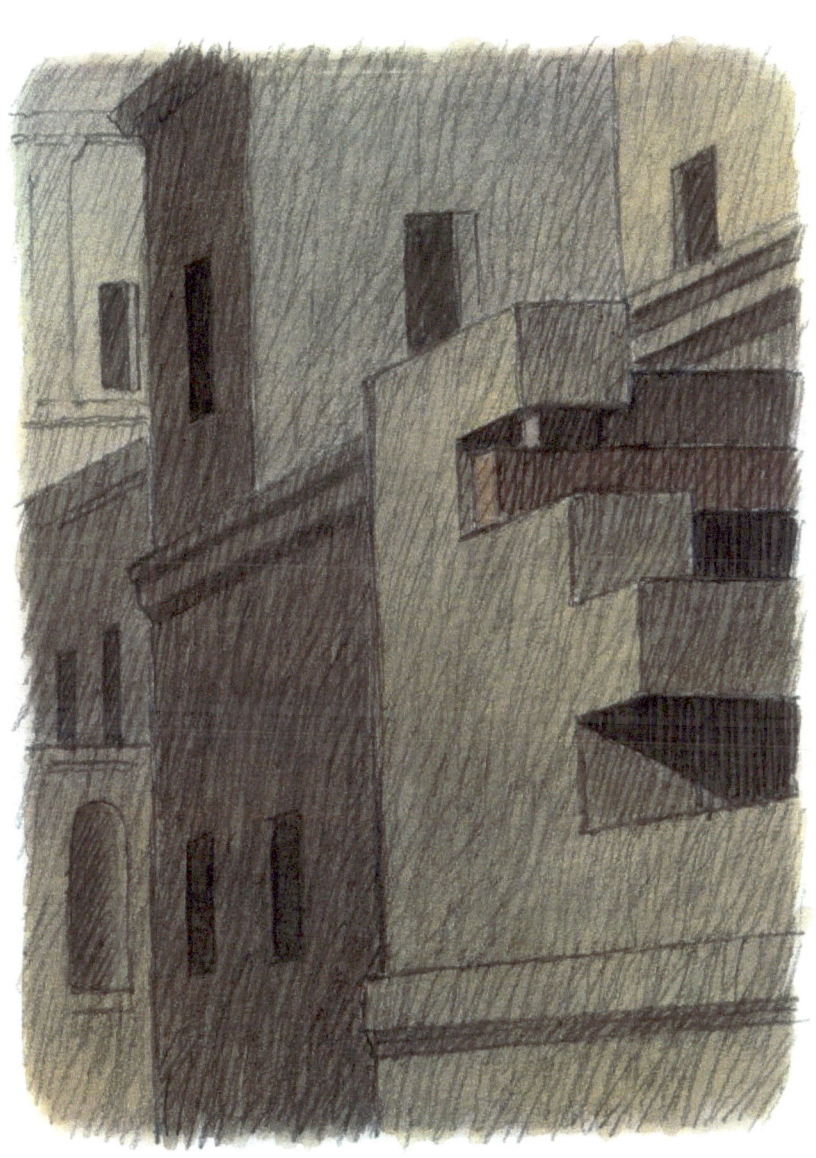

11. Jan Vermeer (1632-75)

Woman pouring milk c. 1660

Rijksmuseum, Amsterdam

Vermeer's paintings have been described as still life pictures with human beings in them. Certainly, he lavishes as much of his technical brilliance on humble background objects and surfaces as on his human subjects. This painting is no exception - we look past the maidservant into the corner beyond and find a small theatre of objects lit by a cool, diffused daylight that picks out every detail, but without any harsh edges or angles. In fact, the actual subject of most of Vermeer's paintings, almost regardless of the actual theme or title, seems to be light itself - the cool, even light of the Low Countries. He actually produced very few paintings in his lifetime, and most of them are quite small, but both foreground and background are so exquisitely rendered that they become almost jewel-like. It is still hard to believe that someone with such a gift could have died penniless and remained virtually forgotten for more than two centuries.

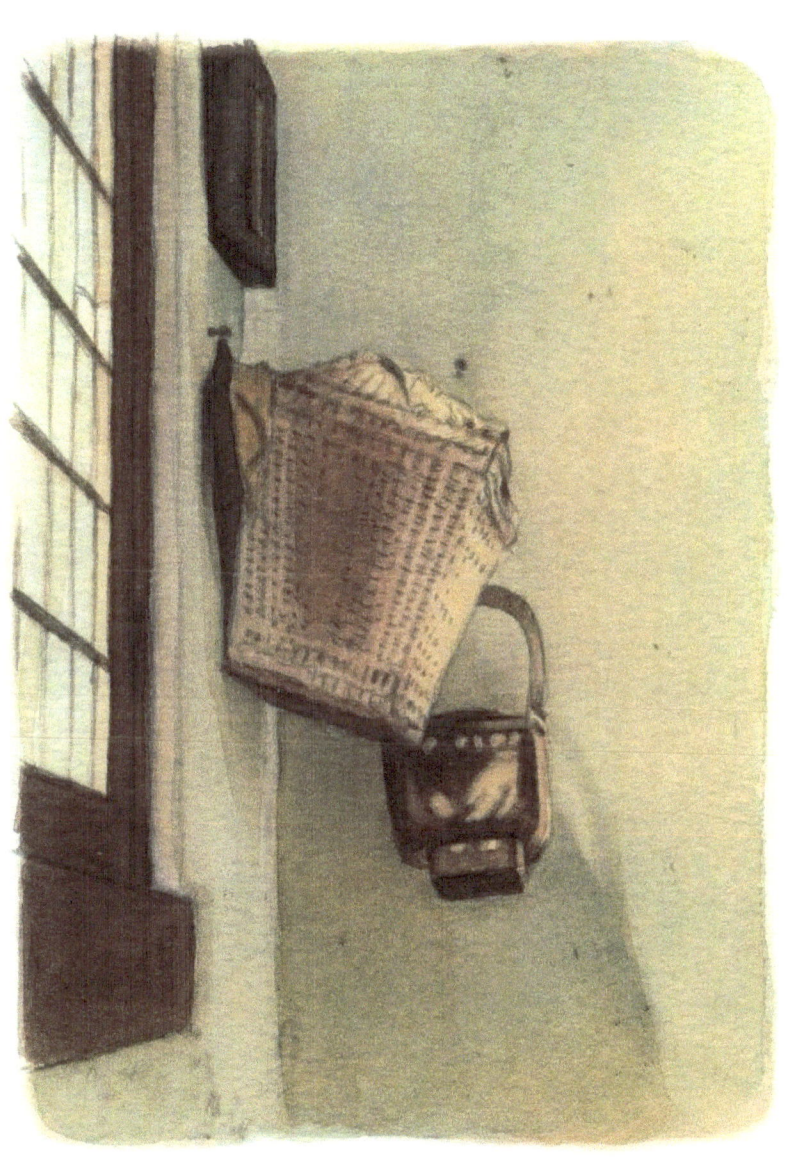

12. Francois Boucher (1703-70)

Venus and Mars surprised by Vulcan 1754

Wallace Collection, London

Boucher was one of the great masters of the frivolous Rococo style of the mid eighteenth century. He enjoyed the favour of Mme de Pompadour, the mistress of Louis XV, and this painting may have been intended for her boudoir. An imagined scene of mythological sensuality, it allowed him to show off his supreme talent for painting delectable female flesh and rich, sumptuous fabrics. But Boucher was no realist - rather he was the consummate interior decorator, his designs and colours were always intended to create or add to the opulent interior of a rich and powerful patron - particularly if that patron, like Mme de Pompadour, was fond of soft pale blues, pinks and pastel shades. He did not work from nature, declaring that real landscapes were "too green". He even dispensed with live models later in his life, preferring to work from memory and imagination. So it can be assumed that this glowing background sky, with its billowing clouds almost like Rococo trees, is a caprice, a fantastic invention.

13. Thomas Gainsborough (1727-88)

The Hon. Frances Duncombe 1778

Frick Collection, New York

Gainsborough made his fortune with his dashing, spontaneous portraits of many of the fashionable celebrities of his day. But despite this success, he dreamed all his life of being simply a landscape painter. Unfortunately, there was virtually no market for this genre of painting, which was rather looked down on, not least by Gainsborough's rival, the president of the Royal Academy, Sir Joshua Reynolds. Gainsborough's society portraits are widely praised for his skill at capturing a likeness, and not least for his bravura technique of rendering fine fabrics. But very often, the imaginary backgrounds of his sitters betray his real love - not naturalistic scenery as such, but an idealised, Arcadian vision of landscape, painted rapidly with a delicate, almost feathery style of brushwork. This "dream of nature" (rather than nature itself) frequently involved fragments of classical architecture framed by sinuous foliage, bathed in the dim golden light of a vague antiquity.

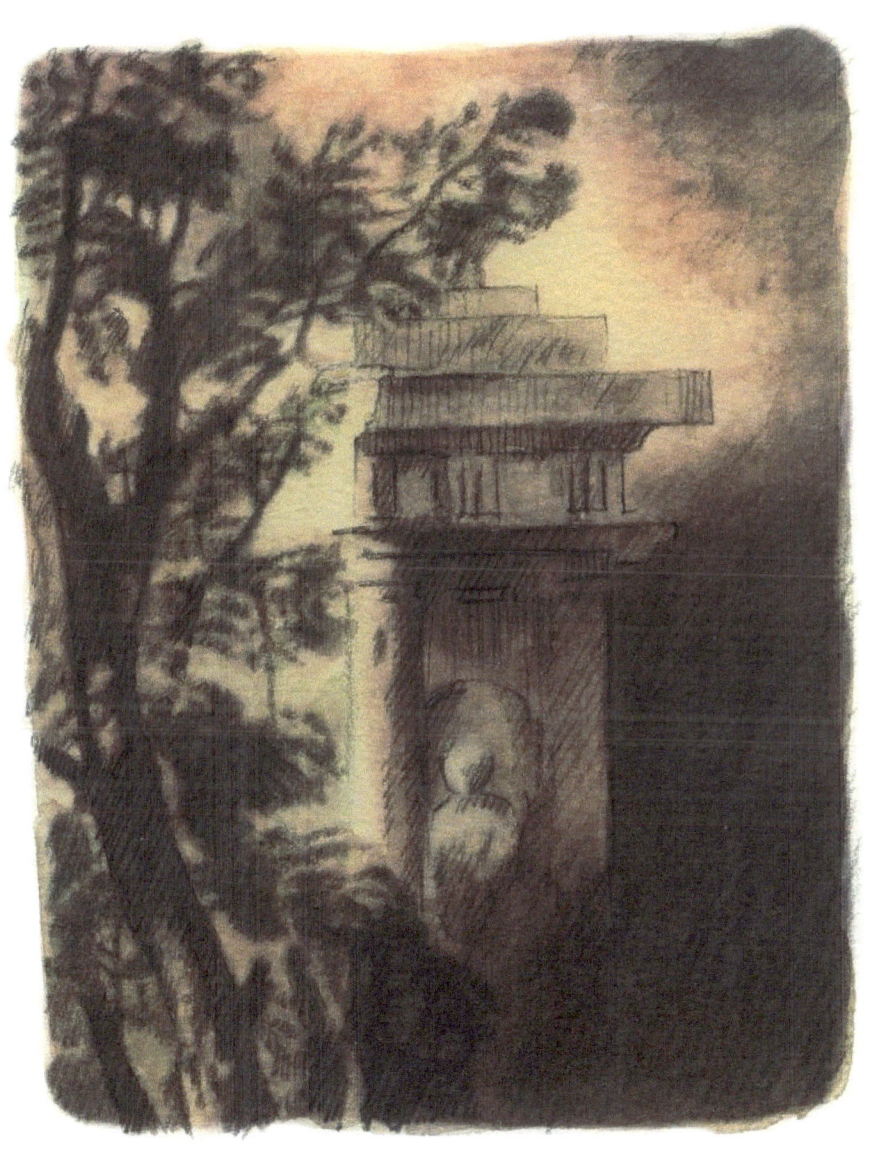

14. Angelica Kauffman (1741-1807)

Lady Elizabeth Foster 1785

Ickworth, Sussex

Though born in Switzerland, Angelica Kauffman became a celebrated artist in several European centres. As was the case with most women artists of this period, she received no formal art training, but acquired her early skills under the tuition of her father, who specialised in murals and portraits. It was as a portraitist that Kauffman became much sought-after throughout Europe; the fact that she was a skilled musician and fluent in at least four languages probably helped. However, she produced some of her most successful work in England where she was befriended by, among others, Sir Joshua Reynolds - she was in fact one of only two women to be named as founders of the London Royal Academy. Influenced by Reynolds, her portraits follow the neoclassical tradition in terms of pose and costume, but there is a delicacy about her touch which is more reminiscent of the Rococo style. This picture, which was begun in Naples but finished in England, is a portrait of a rather notorious English aristocrat. The sitter is seen resting in a shady grove (with overhanging foliage strongly reminiscent of Gainsborough), then beyond her, an idealised landscape with a distant hillside rising above a lake. The dreamlike quality of this background scene gives the image as a whole a gentle, arcadian atmosphere.

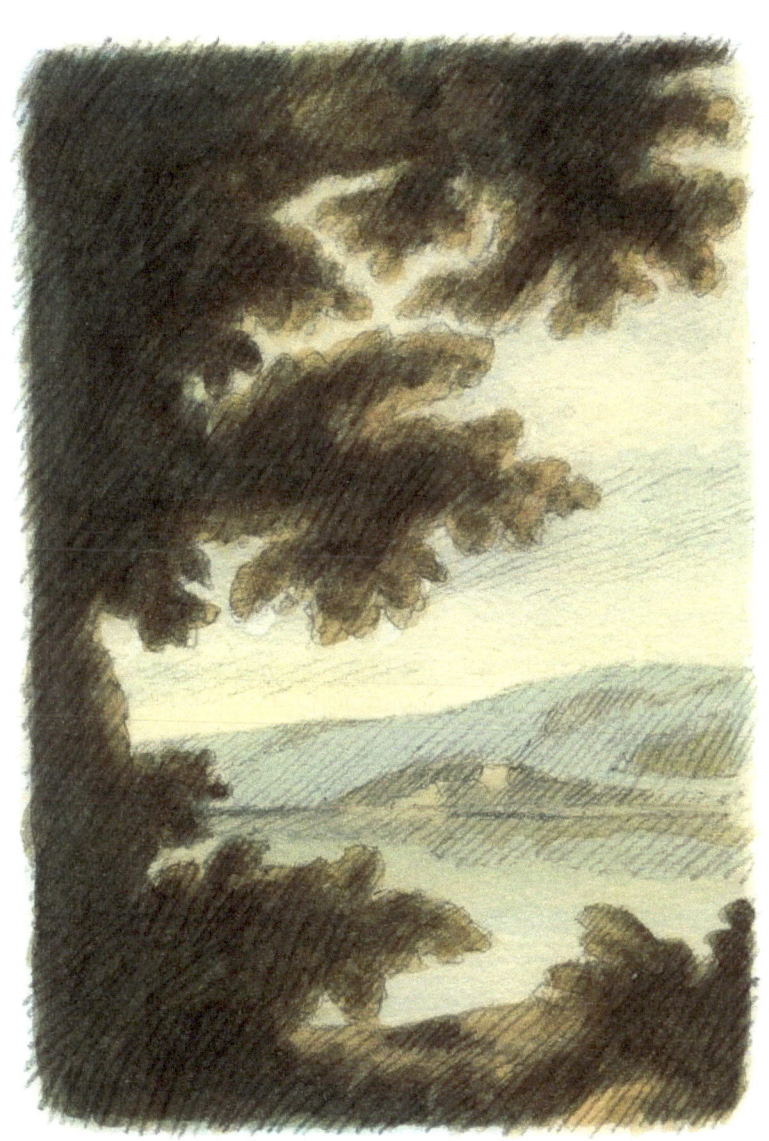

15. Sir Thomas Lawrence (1769-1830)

Queen Charlotte 1789

National Gallery, London

Thomas Lawrence was a spectacularly successful portrait painter from a very early age. He rapidly became a great favourite among the elite of London, as evidenced by the fact that he was given this commission to paint the queen's portrait at the age of only twenty-one. Stylistically, he followed in the footsteps of his heroes of the preceding generation of English portraitists: principally Sir Joshua Reynolds in terms of drawing and composition, but also Thomas Gainsborough in his lively, fluid handling of oil paint, particularly in depicting silks and expensive fabrics. The basic elements of the background of this picture - a vertical columnar panel behind the queen, with swags and pendants of drapery hanging down - are pure Reynolds. The device of an open window looking out on to landscape was also commonly used by Reynolds, but in fact goes much further back to the masters of the Italian Renaissance, particularly Titian. The view we are given is an extensive sweep of countryside looking over Eton towards distant hills, with the all-pervasive browns and muted blues of the period helping to establish the rather grand and solemn character of the image as a whole.

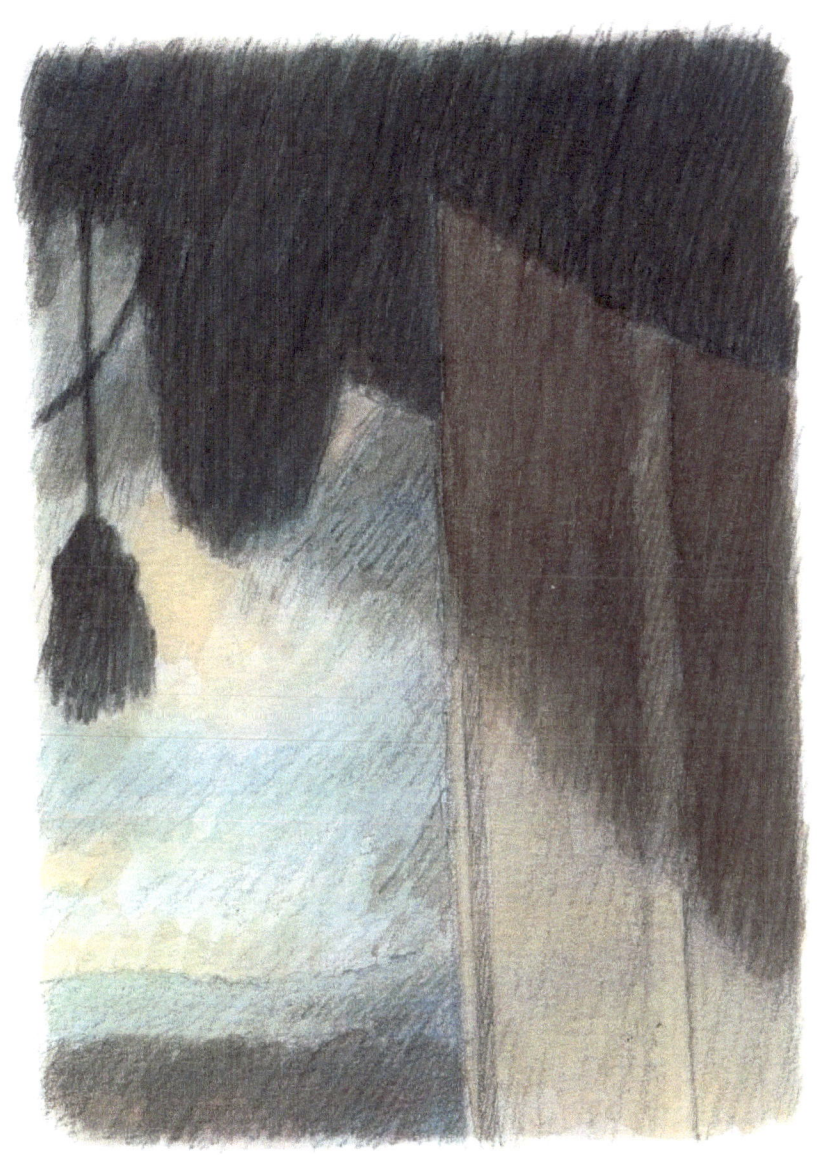

16. Eugene Delacroix (1798-1863)

The Barque of Dante 1822

Louvre, Paris

Delacroix enjoyed early success when this painting was accepted for the Paris salon in 1822. It is a dark and dramatic image taken from Dante's epic poem The Inferno. It depicts Dante's descent into hell guided by the Latin poet Virgil. They stand on a boat crossing the river Styx, with the bodies of the damned floating around them. Delacroix's soft painterly style, influenced by the great line of European colourists including Titian and Rubens, was perfect for such a gloomy, nightmarish subject. But then Delacroix believed that colour was far more important than precise drawing, and that the imagination was more essential to the artist than historical knowledge. In the background of the picture, hell is seen literally as the City of the Damned, with vague buildings blazing and enveloped in dense clouds of smoke.

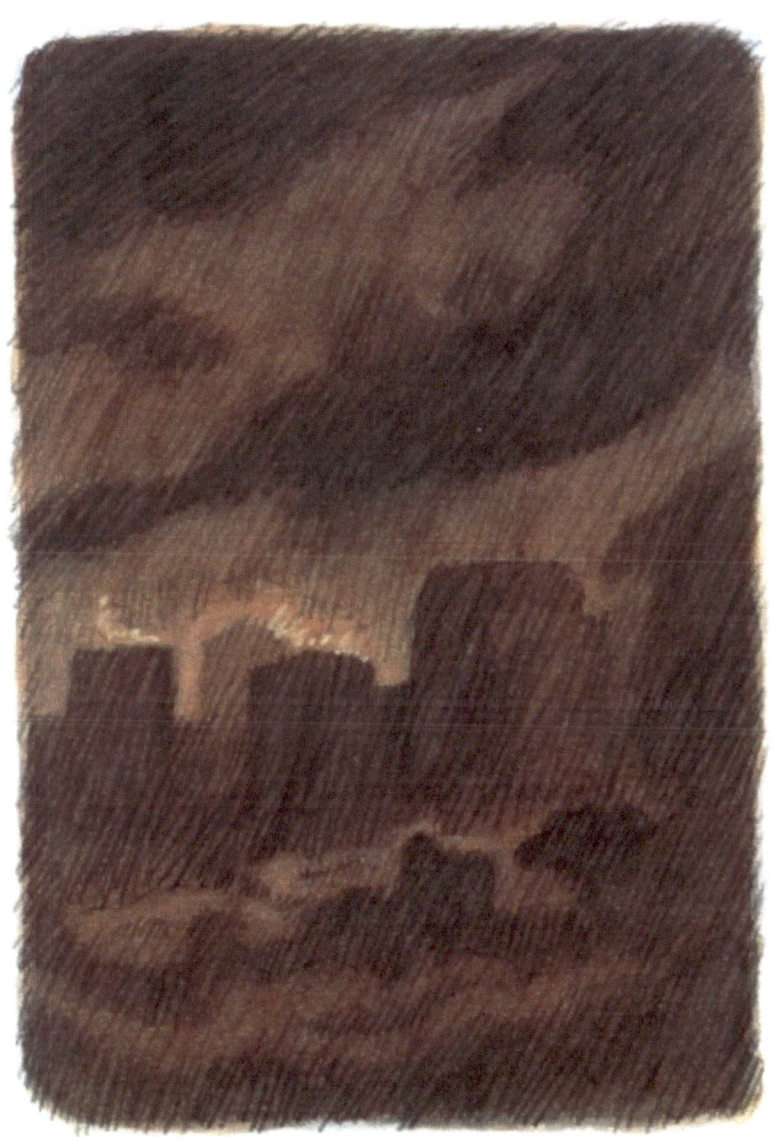

16. Sir Edwin Landseer (1802-73)

The Monarch of the Glen 1851

Private collection, Edinburgh

Queen Victoria's favourite painter, Landseer's reputation soared to tremendous heights during his lifetime, only to plummet as later generations came to regard his work as cloyingly sentimental. But, although his reputation has never really recovered, he remains one of the most skilled and prolific painters of animals, especially dogs. Though in his day he was most famous for his amusing anecdotal pictures of animals and dogs, such as "Dignity and Impudence", to a more modern sensibility "The Monarch of the Glen" remains his most respected image, possibly because (despite the title) it does not attempt to 'humanise" the creature in a superficially entertaining way, unlike many of his other paintings. The background - a blend of the real and the imagined - clearly reflects his genuine love of the landscape of the Scottish highlands. The rocky outcrop, partially obscured by mist, gently evokes the beauty and drama of this noble creature's habitat.

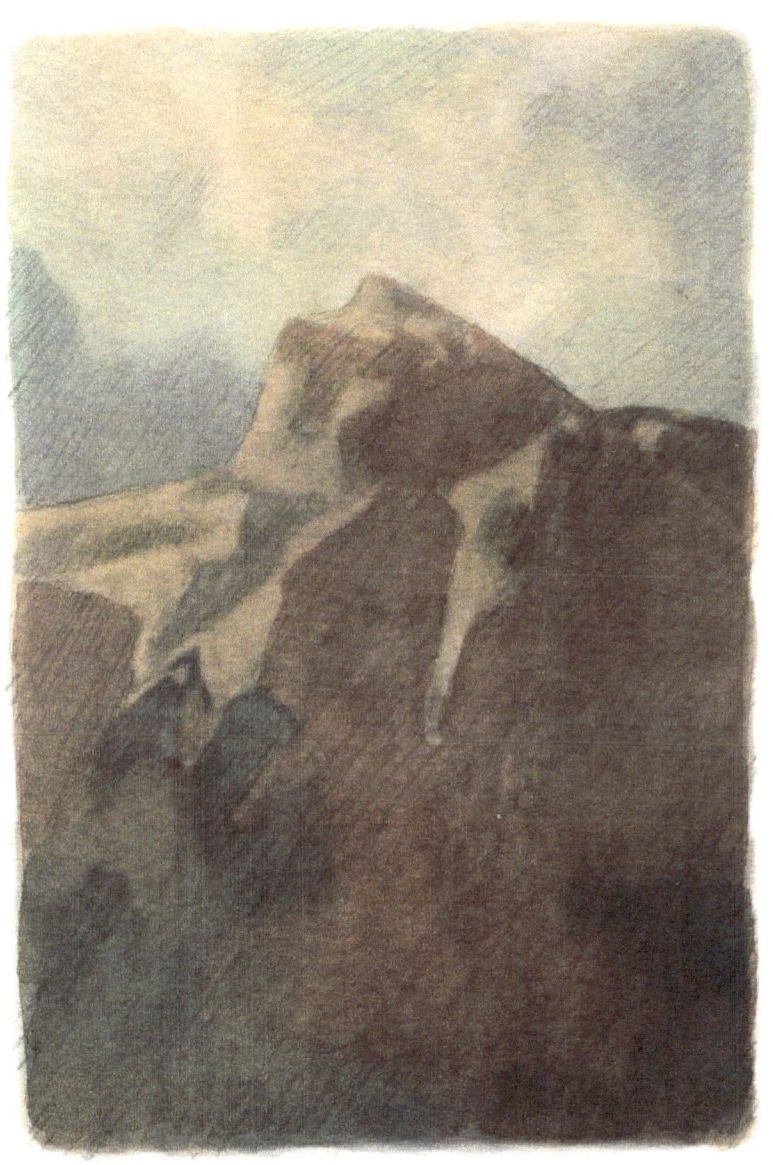

18. Edouard Manet (1832-83)

A café on the Place du Theatre Francais c.1876

Burrell Collection, Glasgow

Although he was regarded as a radical, even revolutionary artist in his time, Manet actually spent much of his life attempting to combine classical approaches to painting with subjects from contemporary life. Yet at the same time, he rejected the fine grading of tones as in the work of many of the old masters in favour of strong, even harsh contrasts of light and shade. Using a spontaneous, impulsive brushwork he had learned from the study of e.g. Frans Hals and Velazquez, he used a lot of black in his earlier work, but later dropped it to adopt the much lighter palette used by the younger Impressionist group. He sketched constantly in the cafes of Paris, as his friend Degas had done. This picture has the feel of a rapid sketch - there is little action, just a woman seated at a table, and a waiter with his back turned. But almost half of the picture surface consists of reflections and these present us with a broad, almost abstract composition of soft, blurred forms. This heightens the feeling of light and space in an otherwise cramped corner of the café, and this soft, vague play of forms and colours are a perfect subject for his use of pastel.

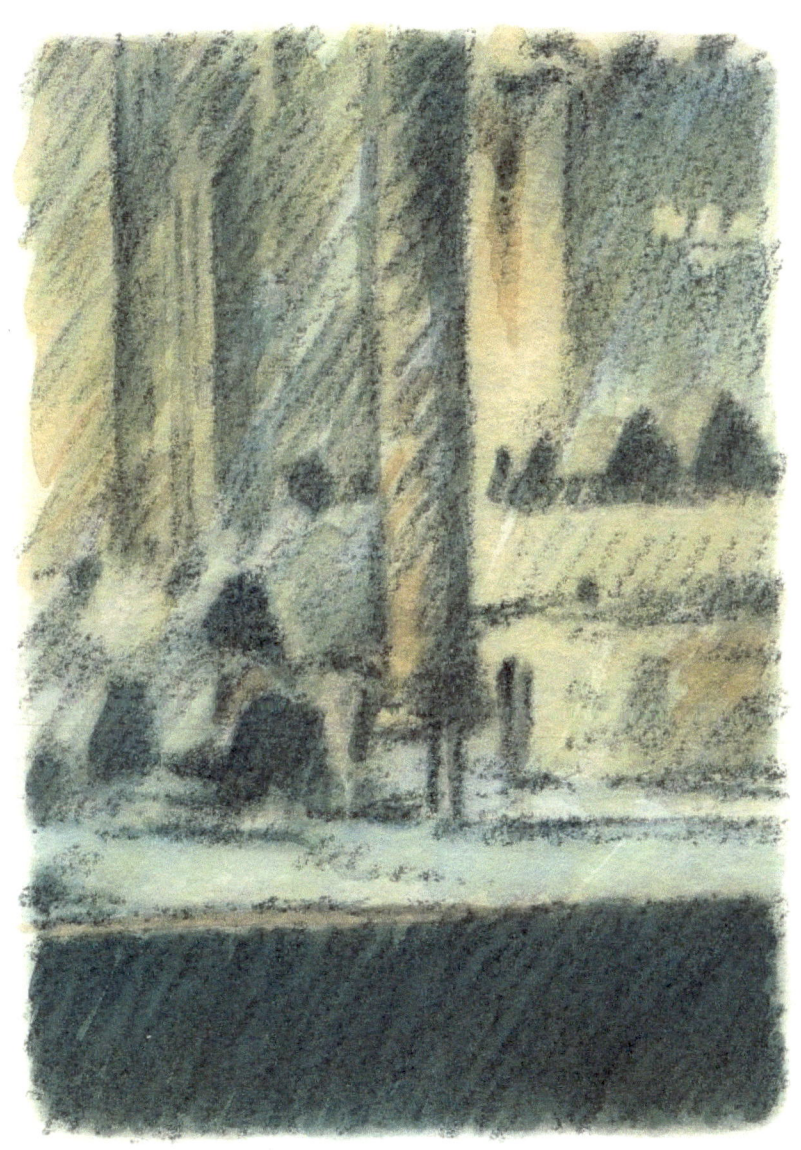

19. Camille Pissarro (1830-1903)

Crystal Palace, London 1871

Private collection, Chicago

Pissarro and his family lived for a time in Upper Norwood, London, as refugees from the Franco-Prussian war of 1870. Later in the decade, he became one of the founders, in fact in many ways the leader, of the Impressionist movement. But this painting, even at this relatively early date, was radical, even revolutionary, with its loose, atmospheric echoes of the work of his hero Corot. The Crystal Palace had recently been moved from Hyde Park to Sydenham, not far from where Pissarro was living. It was a daring subject to tackle for a painter who had previously dealt mainly with open-air landscape. But this detail is from the opposite side of the picture and, in its own quiet way, is just as radical a subject. It depicts a street of fairly recently built middle class villas such as were springing up in many London suburbs - a scene that most people of the time would not look at twice, and certainly would not consider suitable subject matter for art. But with his rapid, spontaneous brushwork capturing the gentle, rather shady light of that side of the street, Pissarro summarises the unassuming, everyday drama of the new Victorian suburbia.

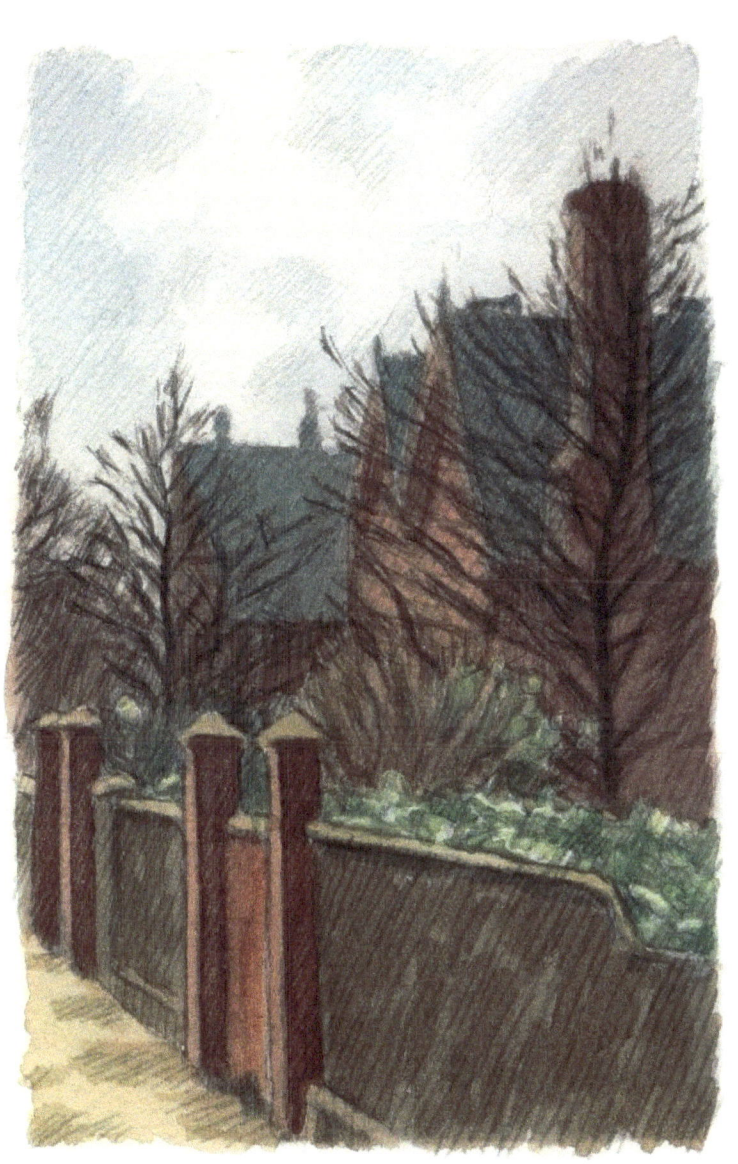

20. Winslow Homer (1836-1910)

Looking out to Sea 1881

Fogg Art Museum, Harvard

Later regarded as one of the greatest American painters, Winslow Homer, at this stage in his career, was still finding his feet as an artist, having only recently emerged from what he regarded as the comparative drudgery of commercial illustration. He had spent some time in Paris studying the work of Edouard Manet and the early Impressionists, but he really began to carve out his personal approach - particularly in the comparatively unforgiving medium of watercolour - during a year which he spent in the small fishing village of Cullercoats on the north east coast of England. There he produced a series of profound watercolour paintings concentrating, as here, on the people, particularly the women, of the local fishing community. In this picture he portrays two of the women in a natural yet heroic pose, standing on the rocks looking out to sea, waiting for the boats to return. Beyond them, we see we see a lowering, rain-filled sky with, across the strip of sea, a dim outline of Tynemouth castle and priory, and in the foreground the solid, rugged rocks of the seashore. All of this is executed in the bold, vivid watercolour strokes which were to become Homer's unique style. The colours of the distant sky and sea are muted and atmospheric, but the foreground rocks are clear and strong - which rather gives the lie to a word of advice he once gave to a young artist: "…..leave rocks for your old age, they're easy".

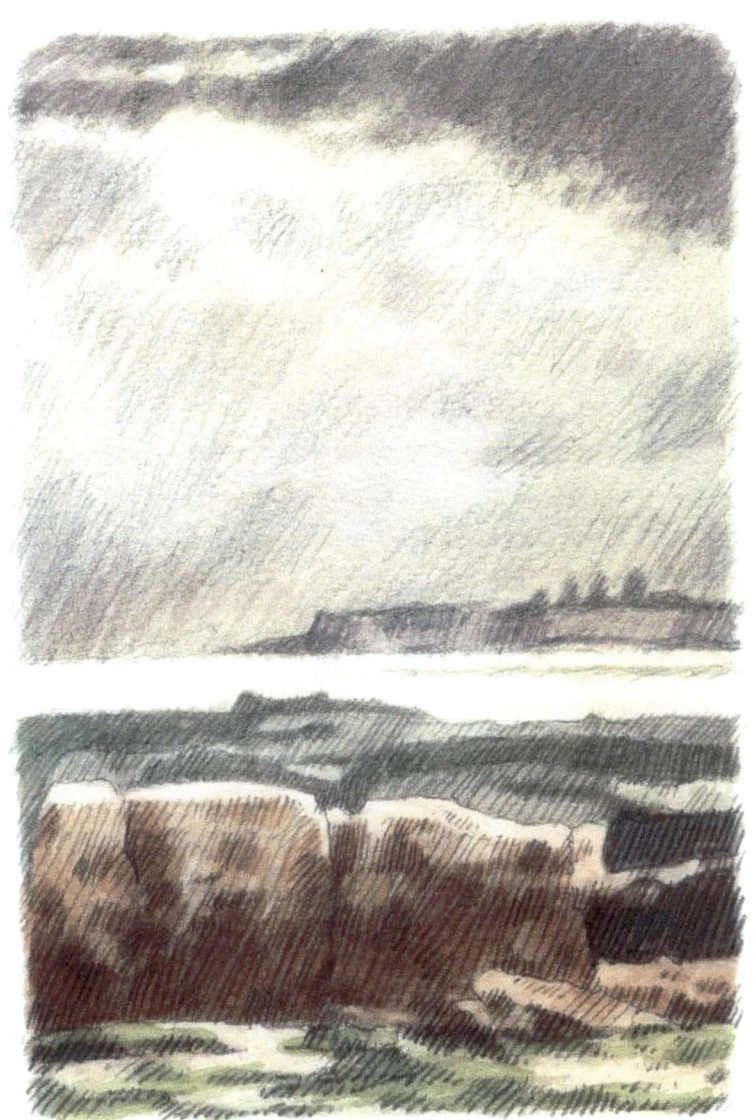

21. Vincent Van Gogh (1853-90)

Garden with Flowers 1888

Metropolitan Museum of Art, New York

Van Gogh's life story is so well known as to have become almost a cliché. Largely self-taught as an artist, he came to painting by way of several failed attempts at other occupations during his early years in Holland and, briefly, in England. But as a painter - supported by his devoted brother Theo - he first imbued the principles of Impressionism during his time in Paris. Then, in an amazingly short period, his artistic development and indeed his sheer output became quite staggeringly sure and rapid. But above all it was his move to Arles in the South of France, especially during his almost magical year of 1888, that brought about the unprecedented transformation of his style and vision. Often producing at least two paintings a day out in the blazing sun, he captured the intense light and colour of the south in a unique way - his compositions influenced by his love of Japanese prints, and his brushwork developing an almost sculptural quality. But even at this stage, his mental state was becoming fragile, which eventually resulted in his admission to a mental hospital and ultimate suicide in 1890. Nevertheless, he went on producing remarkable paintings like this one. This particular detail offers us a sun-drenched vignette of a house at the end of a garden filled with brilliantly coloured flowers, which sums up a statement he made in one of his many letters to Theo: "under the blue sky the orange, yellow, red splashes of the flowers take on an amazing brilliance….." Yet in the garden as a whole, the colour is more dense and solid, reflecting his further statement in the same letter that: "…..instead of trying to reproduce exactly what I have before my eyes, I use colour more arbitrarily, in order to express myself forcibly".

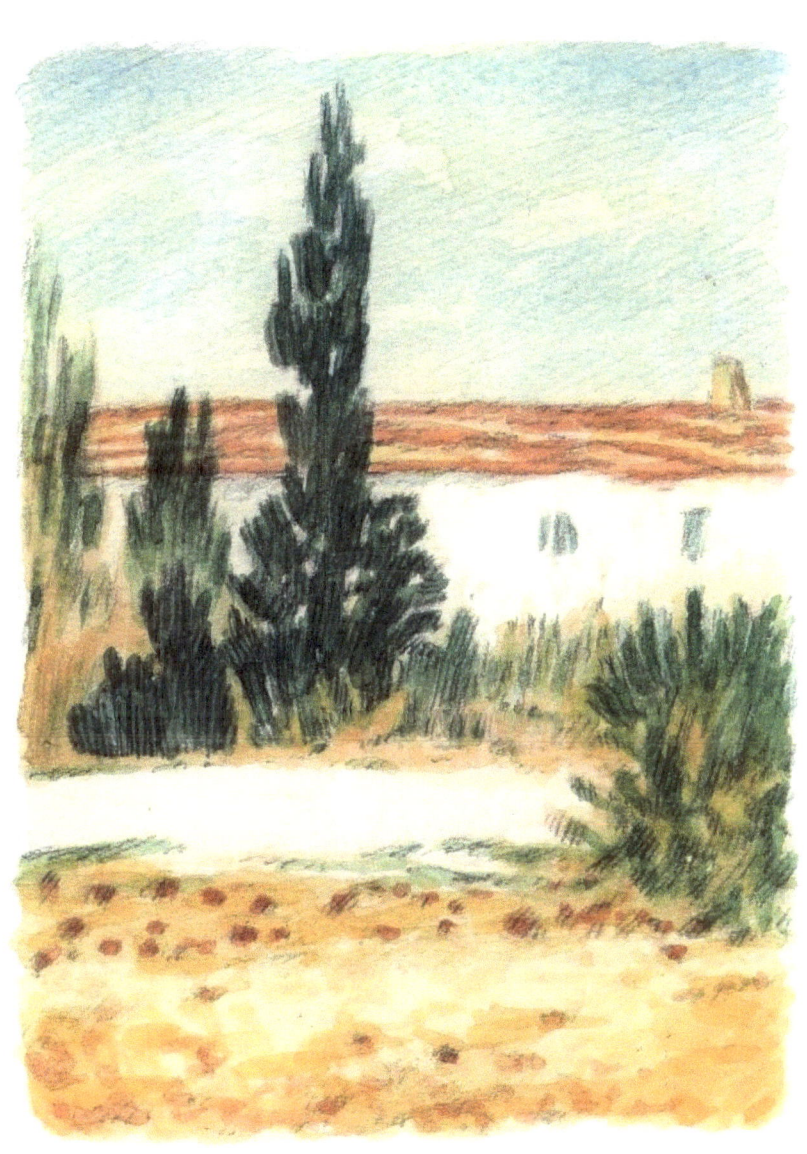

22. Henri Matisse (1869-1954)

Studio, Quai St-Michel 1916

Phillips Collection, Washington

In this picture, we look beyond the model and the studio interior out of the window at the buildings in this corner of Paris. At this stage in his career, Matisse was spending much of the year in the South of France, where the bright, saturated colours he had developed as early as 1906 with Andre Derain and others (which had earned them the nickname of Les Fauves, or "wild beasts") became established. But here he is looking at the relatively grey light of the north. This detail pays lip service to conventional perspective, but in fact Matisse is not interested in depth but in the flat pattern of colours presented by the scene. Also, despite the convincing effect of daylight seen through the window in contrast with the more subdued light in the studio, his painting is not naturalistic. In this case he is more interested in simply placing areas of flat, unmodulated colour against one another, held by the clear lattice work of the drawing. The overall effect is relaxed and casual - there is nothing here to challenge or trouble the viewer - as he himself had described his painting as: ".....something like a good armchair in which to rest....."

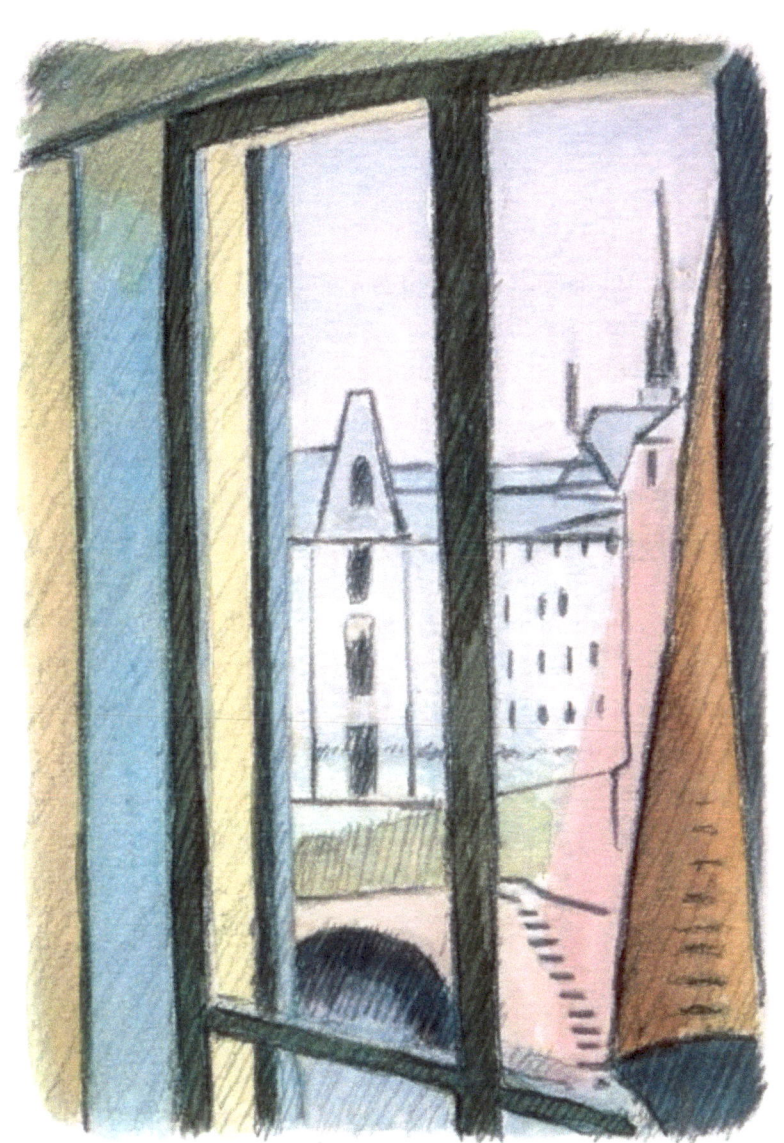

23. Mario Sironi (1885-1961)

Industrial Outskirts 1922

National Gallery, Berlin

This drab, almost menacing scene of massive, impersonal buildings forms part of the backdrop to a strange, enigmatic foreground image featuring a woman holding a baby and confronting a beggar in a space that can only be described as a wasteland. Though not entirely typical of Sironi's work, the roughly handled paint, the brutal monumentality and the sombre colour are all characteristic of his style at this period. At the time, and for some years afterwards, his harsh ungainly figures and settings commanded a good deal of attention. But fashions in art can change rapidly, and his open espousal of Mussolini's fascism meant that he quickly fell out of favour after the second world war. Not surprisingly - given the recurrence of rather grim images in his painting - he suffered from periods of depression and became relatively withdrawn in later life. But this background image, though it could be seen as depressing, could also be considered as an expression of the sad but imposing beauty of the industrial architecture of the early twentieth century.

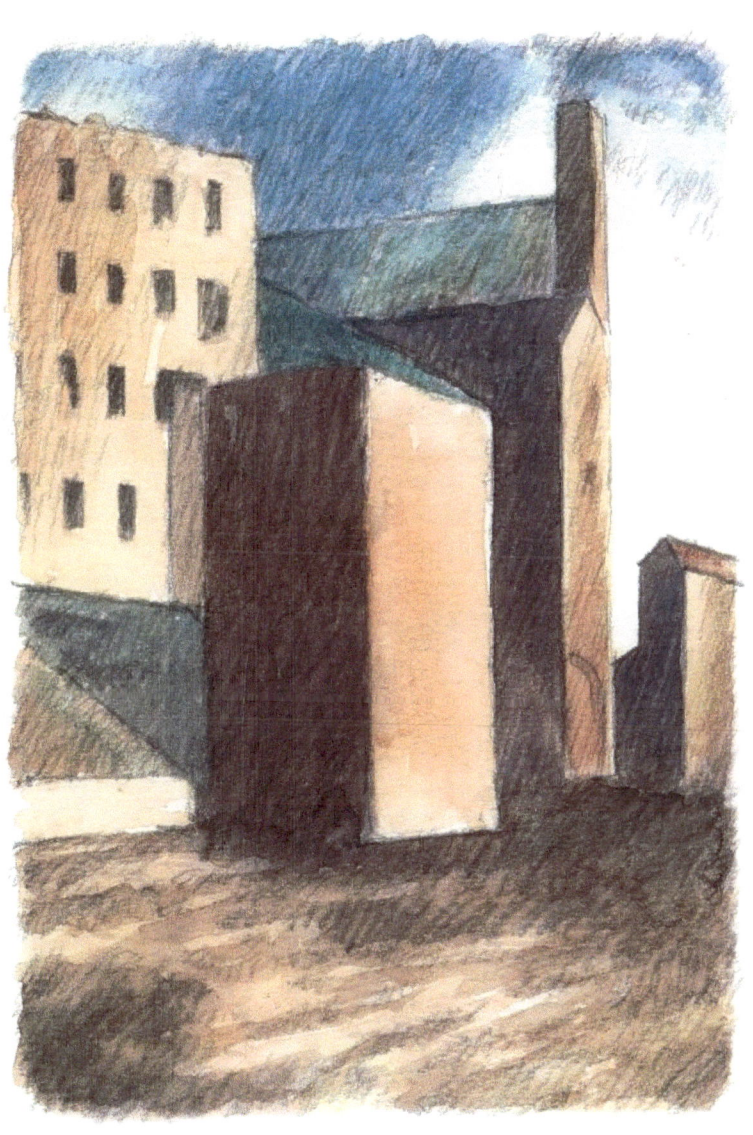

24. Edvard Munch (1863-1944)

The Night Wanderer 1924

Munch Museum, Oslo

Though often referred to as the most important Norwegian expressionist artist, Munch was a unique individual, both personally and in terms of his art. His most famous painting "The Scream" has come to be regarded as the foremost expression of early twentieth century angst. No stranger to disease and death - his mother and sister both died during his adolescence, prompting him to write: "…..illness, madness and death were the black angels who kept watch over my cradle" - he suffered from depression during much of his life. All of which may go some way towards explaining the dark, gloomy, almost forbidding interior in this image. Although it is one of a number of self portraits, the title "The Night Wanderer" speaks volumes about the life of an anxiety-driven insomniac. We look beyond the gaunt figure of the artist into a nondescript section of the room at a window which seems to close off the space rather than suggest anything that might lie beyond this claustrophobic corner. The colours in the painting are strong and vibrant, but at the same time sombre, even oppressive.

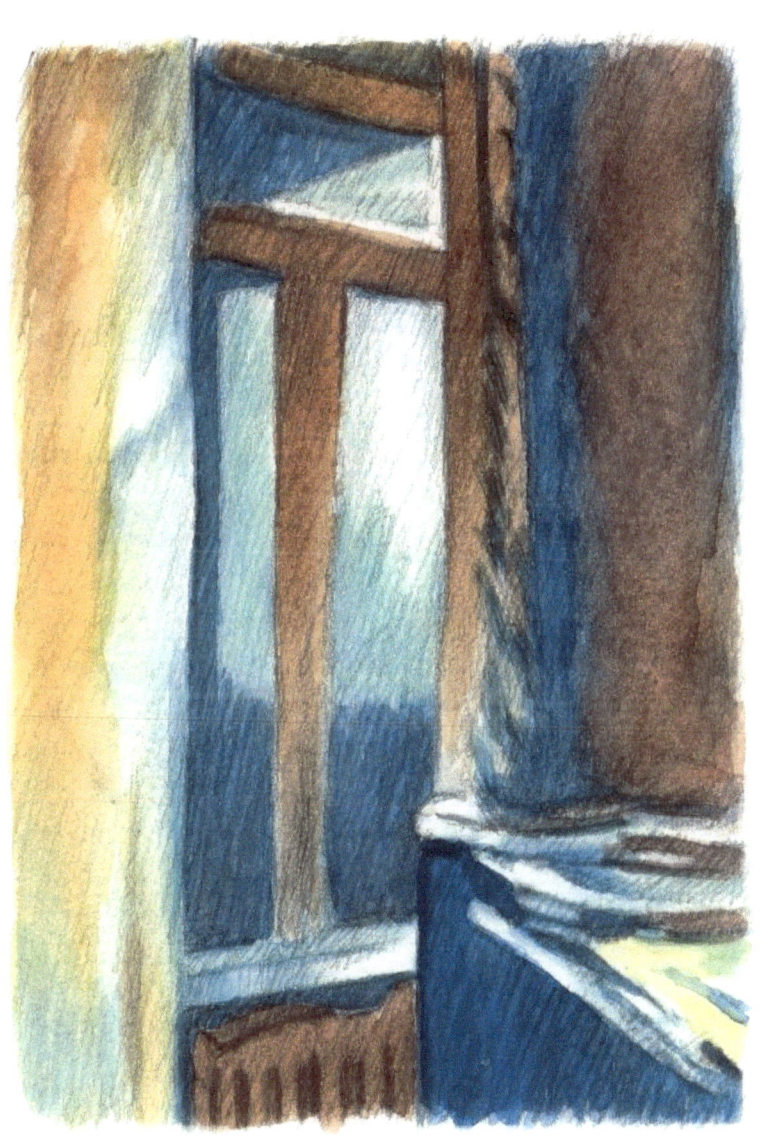

25.Christopher Wood (1901-30)

Zebra and Parachute 1930

Tate Gallery, London

In the background of this painting we get a glimpse of part of the nearly-completed iconic modernist Villa Savoie at Poissy by Le Corbusier. We can readily accept that Christopher Wood admired this revolutionary building, but why he chose to include a zebra and a parachutist in the picture is less easy to decipher. Wood's vision, in his short life as a painter, had always been idiosyncratic, if not childlike, but even so this is a particularly enigmatic image. Wood was born in Liverpool and, in many ways, was quintessentially English, but during the 1920's he spent time in Paris and became acquainted with many of the great early twentieth century modernists. But his style of painting was heavily influenced by his discovery, through his friend Ben Nicholson, of the naïve Cornish painter Alfred Wallis. However, the cool tonality of this background is unlike most of his previous work, which perhaps may be significant in that this was his last painting before his untimely death.

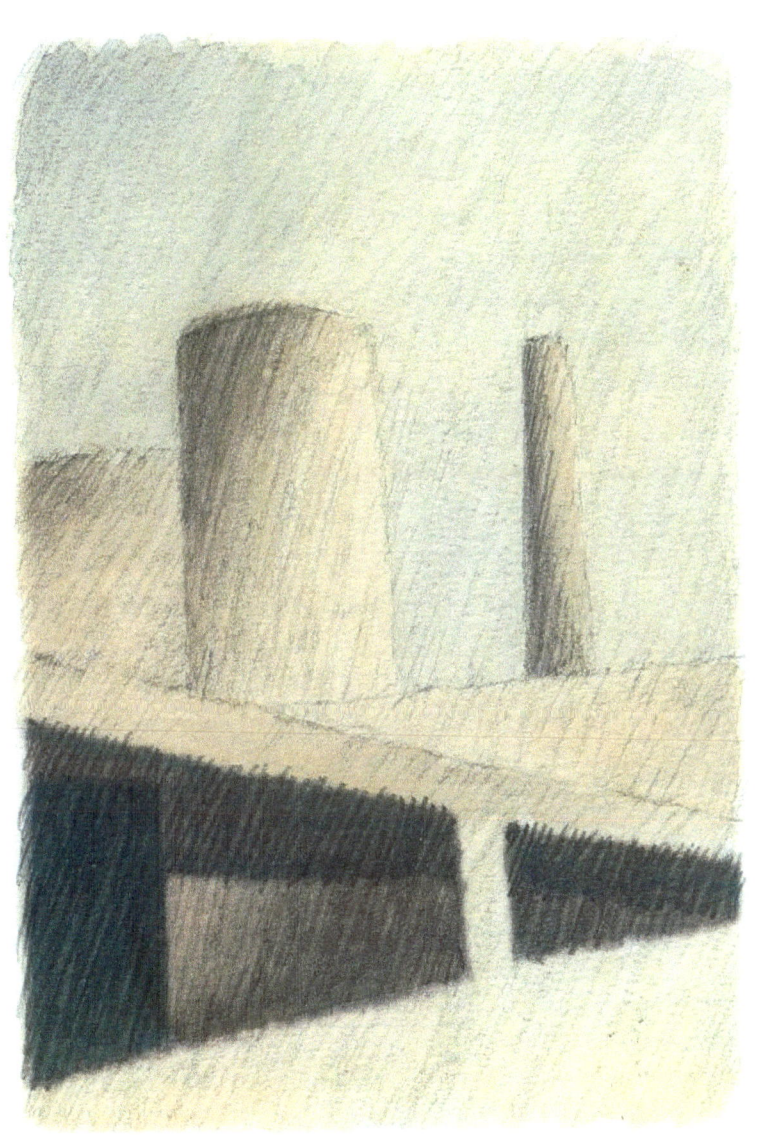

26. L. S. Lowry (1887-1976)

After the Fire 1933

A. J. Thompson Collection

L. S. Lowry lived all of his life near Manchester, mainly in Salford. He worked as a rent collector until his retirement, painting at night in his mother's house, which he did not leave until well after her death. He was a solitary, introverted man, and this was reflected in his paintings: although most of his pictures are crowded with figures, they rarely interact with one another and are depicted in a stark, minimalist way (they are often referred to as "matchstick men"). Most of his major oil paintings are dominated by the urban industrial landscapes of Lancashire, particularly the gaunt, dramatic mill buildings. At first sight, the backgrounds seem drab and featureless, but on closer study they turn out to be extremely subtle and intricately composed, with forms of buildings picked out in a severely limited palette, against a uniformly white or near-white sky. In this picture we see the usual myriad of Bruegel-like figures in the foreground, but behind and above the town's buildings looms the charred hulk of a burnt-out mill, which injects a further note of melancholy into an already strangely subdued (despite the many human figures) scene.

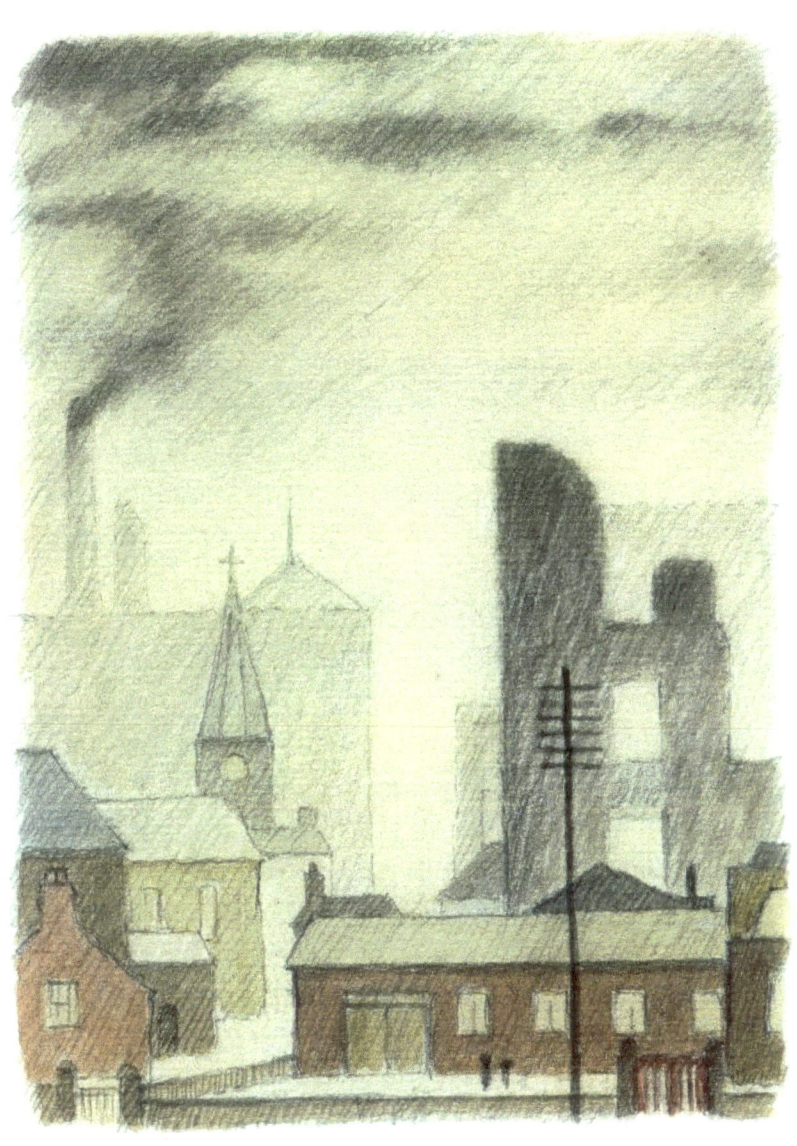

27. Georges Rouault (1871-1958)

Twilight 1939

Metropolitan Museum of Art, New York

In twentieth century painting, Georges Rouault appears a rather solitary yet singular figure. He is often described as an Expressionist, and he was briefly associated with Matisse and the Fauve painters. But there the similarity ends - his work is actually unlike that of any of the early twentieth century Expressionists. He originally trained as a stained glass artist, and the heavy black outlines enclosing often brilliant colours throughout his career suggest that he never really relinquished that initial influence. But his early subject matter was as provocative as any of the German Expressionists. In the first half of his long career he often portrayed downtrodden and marginalised characters such as prostitutes and clowns, but also those who pulled the strings of society, e.g. judges. But he was a devout, if slightly unorthodox Christian, therefore much of his later painting is devoted to religious themes. This picture is usually given the title "Twilight", though it is clearly a Biblical scene, possibly Mary and Joseph seeking a place to give birth. Looking beyond the foreground figures, we see a vaguely middle eastern town, which may be Bethlehem, framed against a sinking, but still bright sun, the forms of the buildings picked out in his characteristically loose but forceful black outlines. These outlines enhance the rich, almost glowing colours to give an other-worldly, distinctly sacred character to the image as a whole.

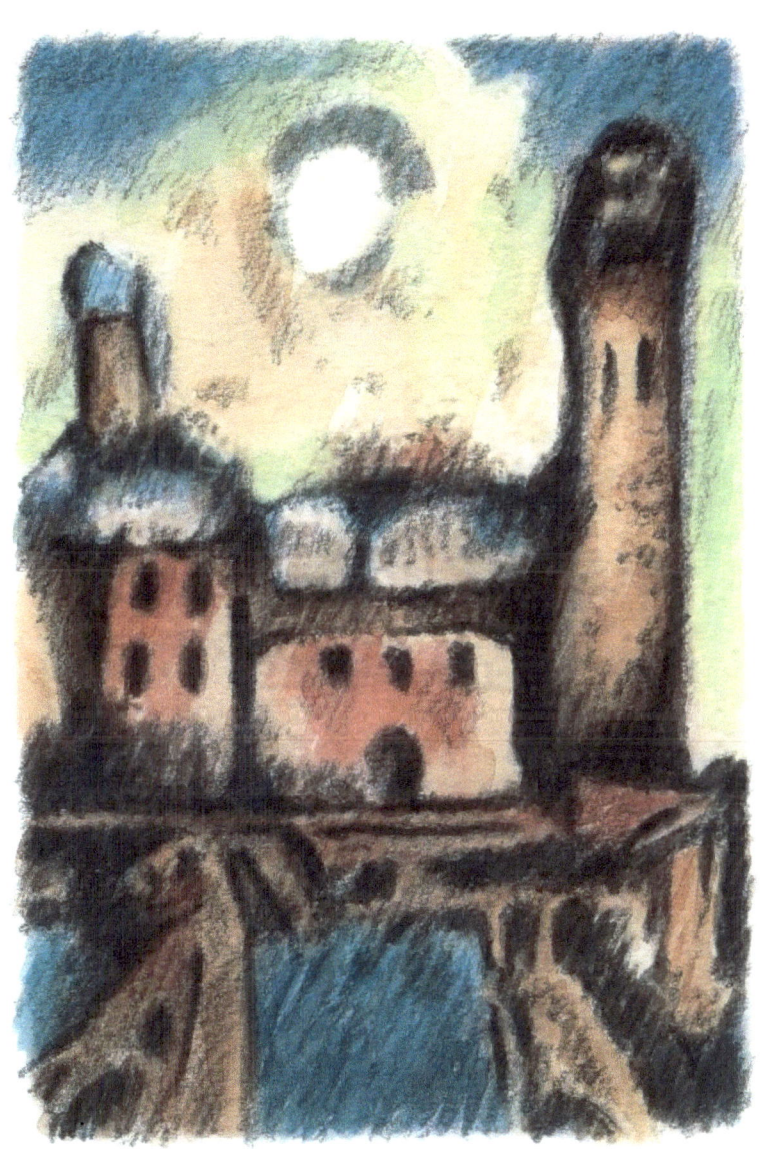

28. Paul Delvaux (1897-1994)

The Staircase 1946

Musee des Beaux Arts, Ghent

The Belgian painter Paul Delvaux is famed for his cool, dreamlike images of beautiful nudes surrounded by strange classical buildings. In his earlier career, he spent time in Italy and was clearly intrigued by classical architecture and sculpture - but not in a literal sense. His buildings are un-constructable, and his female figures often appear to be the same, unattainable dreamlike creature. Although he has come to be regarded as an iconic Surrealist, his work is not at all typical of Surrealism, and in fact he came to the movement relatively late in his career. His distorted perspective and deep dark shadows are reminiscent of De Chirico but, together with the trance-like figures and ambiguous relationships, they add to the vague psychological unease that pervades his work. This detail is in many ways typical of his style - a long, nebulous vista like a recreation of a Roman city, with small, unidentifiable figures receding into a dark, ominous distance. It is almost, but not quite drained of colour, and this contributes further to the indefinably nightmarish quality of the image as a whole.

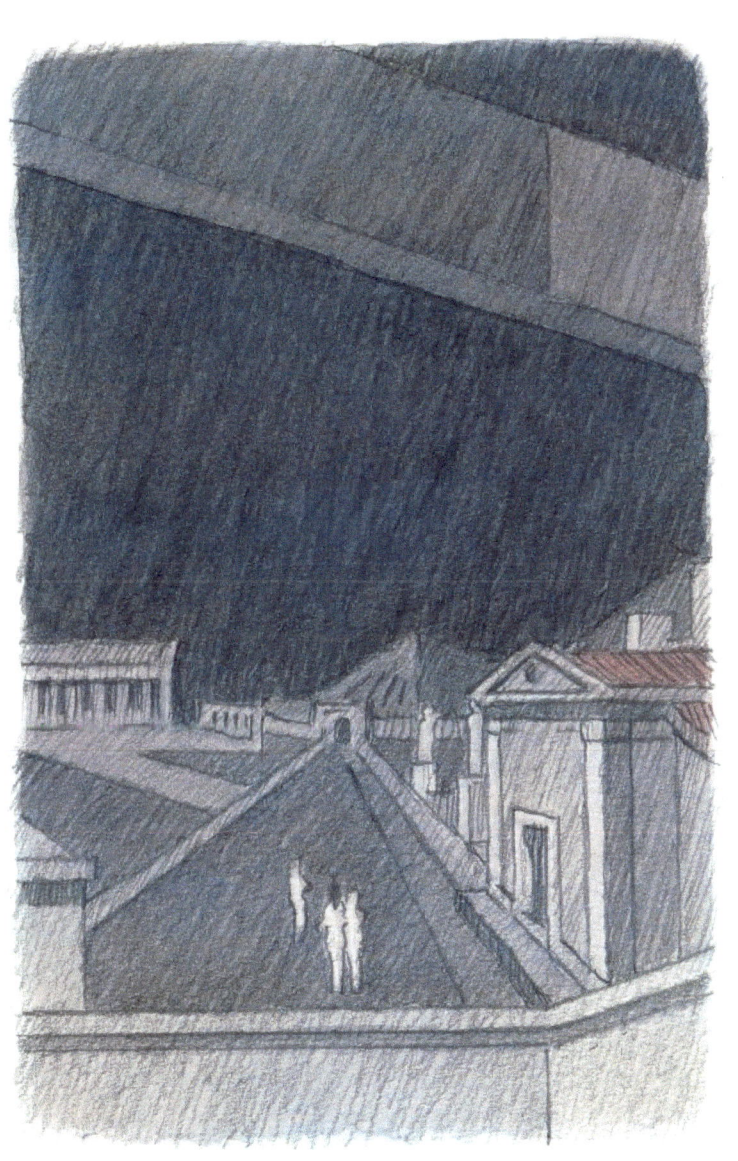

29. Edward Hopper (1882-1967)

Pennsylvania Coal Town 1947

Butler Institute, Ohio

Edward Hopper's painting followed an often solitary path of traditional realism in an era dominated by modernism and abstraction, especially in his native New York. But throughout his life, he sought to find a quiet formal poetry in the most mundane, everyday surroundings of the city. Although he painted figures throughout his career, they often have the appearance of carefully placed models which are there simply to punctuate the chosen scene. His recurrent themes, of comparatively soul-less buildings and empty spaces, have led many critics to conclude that he was essentially concerned with the loneliness of modern life, though he himself said "….the loneliness thing is overdone". A man of very few words, he once said that all he really wanted to do was "….to paint sunlight on the side of a house". Nevertheless, in many of his pictures there is an undeniable sense of detachment on the part of the artist/spectator, and solitude on the part of the figure(s) portrayed. In this painting, a man is raking the lawn between two timber houses. A warm light is streaming on to the side of the houses, which sets up a powerful contrast against the dark shadows on the house frontages. As so often in Hopper's work, the viewer is left wondering what sort of life goes on inside these gaunt facades.

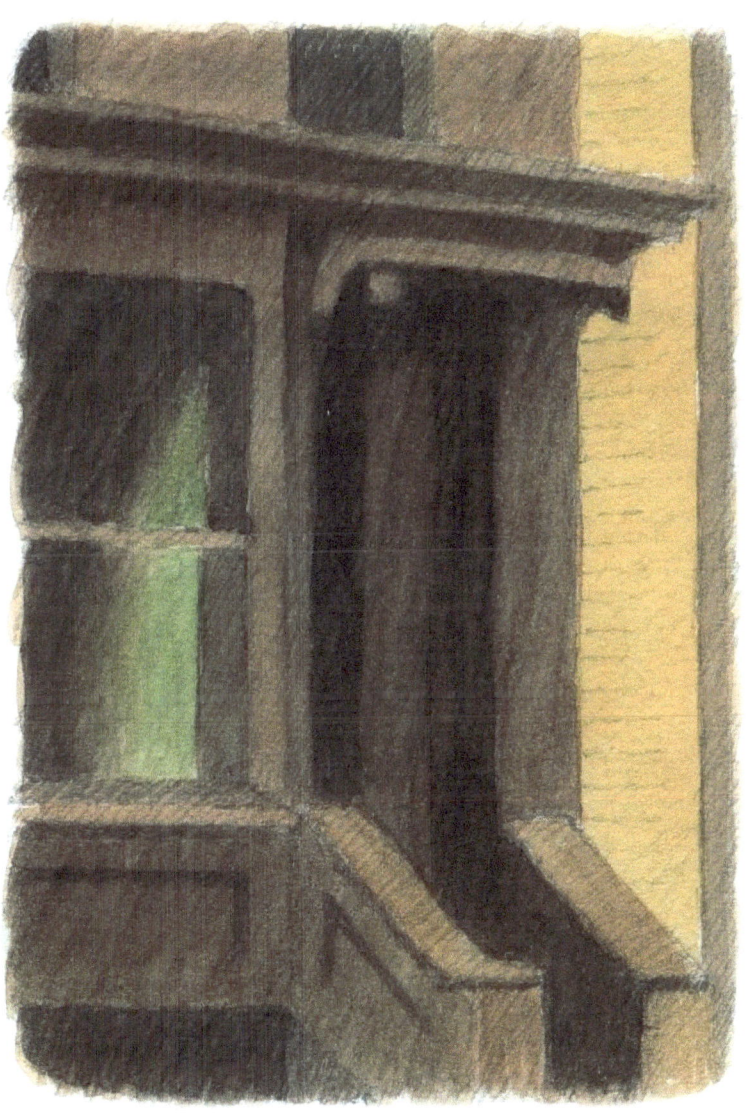

30. Andrew Wyeth (1917-2009)

Up in the Studio 1965

Metropolitan Museum of Art, New York

Whereas so much painting in the twentieth century sets out to challenge our preconceptions about art, Andrew Wyeth's work takes us back to an older, simpler tradition of painting. While much of the century was dominated by modernism and abstraction, he remained a doggedly consistent realist. His art is essentially about ordinary, even mundane rural life in the area near to where he had been born in Pennsylvania. Most of Wyeth's best known mature work is in egg tempera and drybrush, which is a slow and painstaking process. But, however unusual his technique, his work is distinguished above all by his understanding of texture and colour - often tonal and understated, but equally also remarkably rich and varied. Artists throughout the centuries have made use of the device of including a window in the background of the picture, but here Wyeth paints his subject sitting looking directly out of the window - as Edward Hopper had so often done in his earlier New York paintings. In this particular detail, we are made acutely aware of the quality of the daylight entering the darkened studio and the soft, dry surface texture of the wall with its gentle, warm-yet –cool shadows.

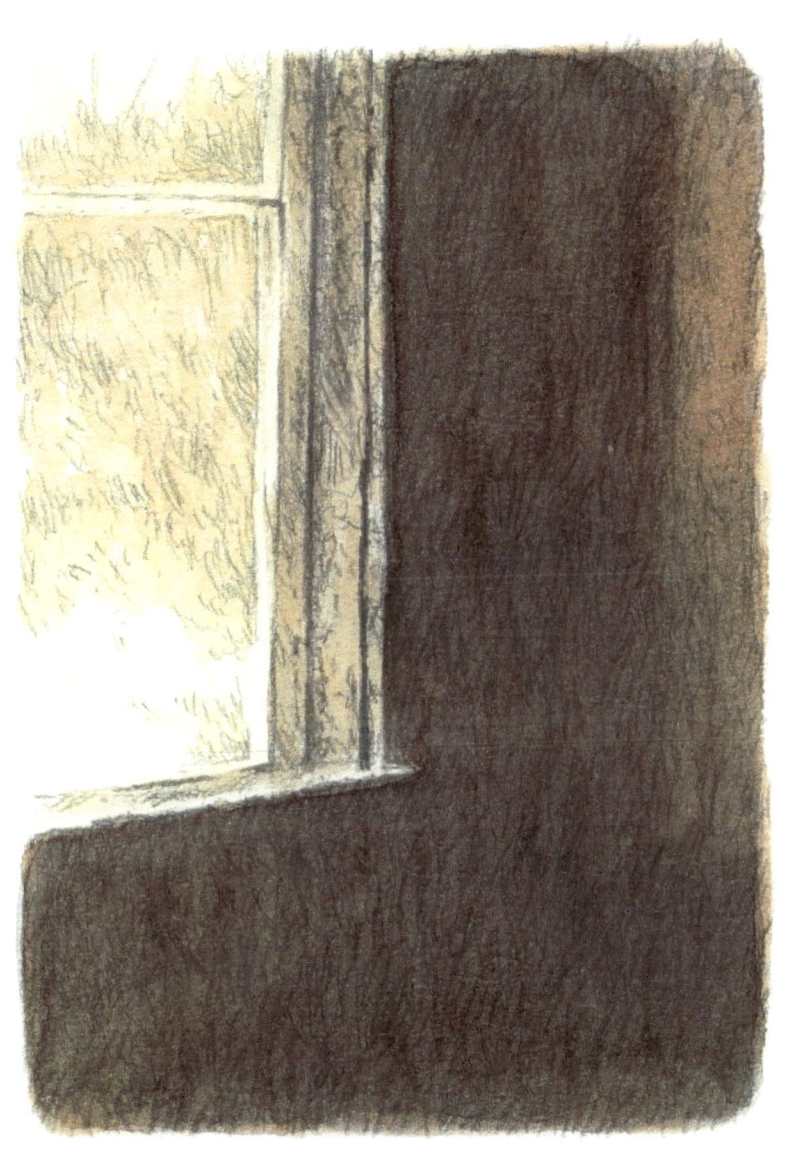